on track ...
Steve
Hackett

every album, every song

Geoffrey Feakes

sonicbondpublishing.com

Sonicbond Publishing Limited
www.sonicbondpublishing.co.uk
Email: info@sonicbondpublishing.co.uk

First Published in the United Kingdom 2021
First Published in the United States 2021

British Library Cataloguing in Publication Data:
A Catalogue record for this book is available from the British Library

Copyright Geoffrey Feakes 2020

ISBN 978-1-78952-098-9

Typeset in ITC Garamond & ITC Avant Garde
Printed and bound in England

Graphic design and typesetting: Full Moon Media

Acknowledgements

A big thank you to Stephen Lambe and all at
Sonicbond Publishing for their support and
encouragement in putting this book together.

Thanks to the Dutch Progressive Rock Page
who have graciously published my album reviews
and interviews since 2005.

Gratitude to Steve and his band members
and associates, past and present.

I would also like to thank all the researchers,
journalists, archivists and fans that have gone before and
made available a wealth of information.

A special thank you to my wife Margaret and her gracious
support through seven months devoted almost entirely to
Mr Hackett, his music and this book.

Would you like to write for Sonicbond Publishing?

At Sonicbond Publishing we are always on the look-out for authors, particularly for our two main series:

On Track. Mixing fact with in depth analysis, the On Track series examines the work of a particular musical artist or group. All genres are considered from easy listening and jazz to 60s soul to 90s pop, via rock and metal.

On Screen. This series looks at the world of film and television. Subjects considered include directors, actors and writers, as well as entire television and film series. As with the On Track series, we balance fact with analysis.

While professional writing experience would, of course, be an advantage the most important qualification is to have real enthusiasm and knowledge of your subject. First-time authors are welcomed, but the ability to write well in English is essential.

Sonicbond Publishing has distribution throughout Europe and North America, and all books are also published in E-book form. Authors will be paid a royalty based on sales of their book.

Further details are available from www.sonicbondpublishing.co.uk. To contact us, complete the contact form there or email info@sonicbondpublishing.co.uk

on track ...
Steve Hackett

Contents

*Geoffrey Feakes has devoted time to comment on all of my
tracks from over the years in this book. Combing through
each album, he expounds his personal view.*
Steve Hackett

Foreword

Steve Hackett first came to my attention when Genesis played the Great
Western Express Festival, Lincolnshire, in May 1972. To be honest, I recall the
persistent rain and mud that blighted the spring bank holiday event more
than I do the performance, but I've remained a fan ever since. A show at the
De Montfort Hall, Leicester on 25 February 1973 during the *Foxtrot* tour was
for me a far more satisfying experience - and for the band I assume because
it was recorded for the subsequent *Genesis Live* album. Steve was already a
fine acoustic and electric guitar player when Genesis took him under their
wing and he swiftly developed into one of the most original, innovative and
influential musicians in rock.

He developed trademark techniques like fast tapping – also known as
hammering or nailing as Steve originally called it. He also pioneered sweep-
picking, finger vibrato, volume pedal swells and sustain using the tremolo arm
and later a sustainer pickup. His harmonic style became synonymous with the
term 'melodic prog', which strongly influenced the British neo-prog bands of
the 1980s and European and Scandinavian neo-neo-prog acts of the '90s. Even
today, he's regularly name-checked in reviews of contemporary artists inspired
by his playing.

Steve's maintained a steady output over a period of five decades with 26
studio albums under his own name, in addition to various collaborations.
While they have not always met with commercial success, he has constantly
strived to avoid the predictable and mundane, creating music with substance
and lasting quality. He has embraced prog-rock, mainstream rock and other
genres such as pop, classical, blues, jazz and world music, all performed with
integrity and a respect for each genre.

With the exception of Anthony Phillips, Steve is by far the most prolific
member of 1970s Genesis in terms of his solo studio album output. His 26
compares with Ant's 33, Peter Gabriel's thirteen, Mike Rutherford's two solo
albums and nine with Mike and the Mechanics, Tony Banks' ten and Phil
Collins' eight. Steve's albums are also arguably the most creative and diverse
and as such, an ideal subject for a book of this kind.

Following the 'Introduction' which includes a brief history of Steve's
career, there is a separate chapter dedicated to each solo album. Every track
is individually discussed in terms of its subject and structure, including a
critical analysis. The tracklisting is from the original UK LP or CD release, while
alternate tracks on releases in other regions such as Japan and America are
included in the 'related tracks' section for each album. Additional tracks on

'special editions' and reissues are also in this section, along with non-album tracks from the same era. I round the book off with a comprehensive overview of his collaborations with other artists, his live albums and compilations of his music. For a detailed analysis of Steve's recordings with Genesis, Stuart Macfarlane's book in the *On Track* series is highly recommended.

A special mention should go to those that have played an important role in Steve's career including Tony Stratton-Smith, John Hackett, John Acock, Nik Magnus, Julian Colbeck, Roger King, Benedict Fenner, Chris Squire and Jo Hackett, as well as all the talented musicians and singers that have shared the same stage and recording studio.

Finally, while I've tried to be as accurate as possible, time and memory can distort the facts, as can unreliable resources. If you spot any errors, please feel free to contact me through the publisher. So read on, I only hope you get as much satisfaction from reading this book as I did writing and researching it.

Geoffrey Feakes, 31 March 2021

Introduction

In 2020, Steve Hackett celebrated his 70th birthday, that age when most of us would consider taking things easy. Not so one of rock's most active musicians. Had it not been for the global effects of the coronavirus, throughout 2020 he would have been touring Genesis' *Selling England by the Pound* and *Seconds Out* albums in their entirety. The North American leg of the world tour was prematurely cut short in March forcing Steve to return to the UK. In the interim period, he kept fans entertained with a succession of video blogs from his home studio. They included solo guitar renditions and 'track-chats' covering some of his and Genesis' most popular songs. He's much more than a heritage act living off past glories however as his impressive solo career testifies.

He was born Stephen Richard Hackett on 12 February 1950 at London's University College Hospital and lived with his family in Pimlico in the heart of the capital. His brother John, born five years later, was also musically gifted. Steve's first instrument, which he mastered at the age of four, was the harmonica, but it was his talents as a guitarist from the age of thirteen that would shape his future. Encouraged by his parents, he listened to a variety of music and like many budding UK guitarists of his generation, he was especially inspired by Hank Marvin of The Shadows. During the British blues boom of the 1960s, acts like John Mayall's Bluesbreakers with Peter Green, the Rolling Stones and Jeff Beck left their mark on the teenage Hackett, as did the Beatles. He was also impressed by American blues guitarist Mike Bloomfield when he toured the UK with the Paul Butterfield Blues Band in the mid-60s.

King Crimson's 1969 debut album was a 'eureka' moment for Steve, as was the explosive talents of Jimi Hendrix. After serving his apprenticeship in proto-prog bands Canterbury Glass, Heel Pier and Sarabande, in 1970 he and John joined Quiet World, led by the Heather brothers John, Lee, and Neil. Steve played on their only album *The Road* and although he didn't contribute any material, the writing and philosophy of the brother's father, in particular, left an impression on the guitarist.

Steve had been placing ads in the music weekly *Melody Maker* for sometime, one of which, in December 1970, has become part of Genesis folklore. It caught the attention of Peter Gabriel and he and Tony Banks auditioned Steve at the Pimlico flat he shared with John. Impressed by his twelve-string guitar playing and fluid technique, Steve was hired in January 1971 as a long term replacement for Anthony Phillips who had left Genesis six months earlier. Stopgap guitarist Mick Barnard had been with the band for just three months before stepping aside for Steve. They had also recently recruited a new drummer and the team of Gabriel, Banks, Hackett, Mike Rutherford and Phil Collins went on to produce some of the most inspirational music of the 1970s.

Following four studio albums with Steve – *Nursery Cryme* (1971), *Foxtrot* (1972), *Selling England by the Pound* (1973) and *The Lamb Lies Down on Broadway* (1974) – Gabriel left the band in 1975 to pursue a solo career. That same year, Steve enjoyed his own taste of solo success with his debut album

8

Voyage of the Acolyte. He returned to the Genesis fold for the pivotal *A Trick of the Tail* album in 1976, but friction surfaced during the recording of the follow-up *Wind & Wuthering.* Steve had become increasingly frustrated when his compositions were sidelined in favour of material from the other band members. He also believed that the success of his solo album was perceived by his colleagues as a threat to the band's stability. By Steve's understandable logic, now the band was a four-piece, his compositions should occupy one-quarter of the album. The other three disagreed and despite a handful of writing credits, his main contribution to the album remained the brooding 'Blood on the Rooftops', co-written with Collins.

He hung around for the subsequent tour and the 1977 *Spot the Pigeon* EP which included the superb 'Inside and Out', his Genesis swansong. With a desire for greater artistic control and unable to endure the protracted process of mixing the *Seconds Out* live album, he left the band in the autumn of 1977. He was certainly taking a gamble, as in the 1977 *Melody Maker* reader's poll, Genesis were voted 'Top British Band' and 'Best Live Act In The World'.

Energised by his newfound freedom and as the 'captain of his own ship', Steve released three successful albums – *Please Don't Touch!, Spectral Mornings* and *Defector* – in as many years. Despite prog-rock becoming decidedly unfashionable in the late 1970s, they were all excellent examples of the genre, backed by sell-out tours from 1978 onwards. Although his 1981 album *Cured* was another success, its mainstream, AOR style divided fans – and your author was not immune. Like many acts from the 1970s, Steve's star shone less brightly in the '80s although he had a minor hit with the single 'Cell 151'. Solo albums continued and unexpected Stateside success came in 1986 with the 'supergroup' GTR and a hit single 'When the Heart Rules the Mind'.

The 1990s saw an artistic – if not totally commercial – return to form for Steve with a run of excellent albums and tours that continued into the new millennium. He revived the classic 1970s material of his former band with *Genesis Revisited* in 1996 and the inevitable follow-up in 2012, backed by extensive world tours and several live releases. More than any other member of the band, Steve has kept the Genesis flag flying. His own music was even more eclectic in the 2010s and his appreciation of world music, in particular, blossomed, culminating in arguably his most impressive studio album *At the Edge of Light* in 2019.

Despite 2020 marking Steve's 70th birthday, there was no sign of him consigning his Les Paul to the attic just yet, and following postponed dates in 2020, both Steve and a reformed Genesis with Collins, Banks and Rutherford planned tours for 2021/2022.

Voyage of the Acolyte (1975)

Personnel:
Steve Hackett: electric and acoustic guitars, Mellotron, harmonium, bells, autoharp; vocals on 'The Hermit', effects
John Hackett: flute, ARP synthesiser, bells
Mike Rutherford: bass guitar, bass pedals, fuzz twelve-string guitar
Phil Collins: drums, vibes, percussion; vocals on 'Star of Sirius'
John Acock: Elka synthesiser, Mellotron, harmonium, piano
Additional personnel:
Sally Oldfield: vocals on 'Shadow of the Hierophant'
Robin Miller: oboe and cor anglais on 'Star of Sirius', oboe on 'The Hermit'
Nigel Warren-Green: cello on 'The Hermit'
Percy Jones: additional bass guitar on 'A Tower Struck Down'
Johnny Gustafson: bass guitar on 'Star of Sirius'
Produced by: Steve Hackett, John Acock
Engineered by: John Acock
Recorded at: Kingsway Recorders, Kingsway, London
Recording date: June – July 1975
Release date: 1 October 1975
Record label: UK: Charisma Records, USA: Chrysalis Records
Highest chart places: UK: 26, USA: 191
Running time: 40:52

In 1975, this was an essential purchase for Genesis fans. Not only did it bridge a gap while the band were taking stock following the departure of Peter Gabriel, but the rich arrangements, colourful instrumentation and strong melodies had a comforting familiarity. It also had the distinction of being the first solo album by a member of the band. Steve's predecessor Anthony Phillips left Genesis in 1970, but he had yet to release his debut album.

Steve based the album's overarching concept on Tarot cards, the same subject chosen by fellow symphonic-rockers The Enid for their 1976 debut *In the Region of the Summer Stars*. More specifically, it relates to a spiritual journey in which each card becomes a metaphor for the characters and emotions experienced along the way. To bring it to life, he engaged several guest musicians – including his brother John – with traditional instruments like flute, oboe and cello playing a key part in the album's arrangements. John also helped out by producing guitar and flute demos using his reel-to-reel tape recorder. With the Genesis rhythm engine of Mike Rutherford and Phil Collins onboard, Steve revealed how great it was to work with them outside the confines of the band. On later albums, he would employ the services of other Genesis associates like Chester Thompson, Anthony Phillips, Bill Bruford and Ray Wilson.

Steve wrote the songs over a period of about a year making good use of nights spent in hotel rooms during *The Lamb Lies Down on Broadway* tour. On the eve of the tour in October 1974, Steve injured his hand and the UK

dates – including the Birmingham show, for which I had a ticket – were
postponed. At a reception for the Sensational Alex Harvey Band, someone
commented that the band would be nothing without Alex and in Steve's mind,
they could have been talking about Genesis and Gabriel. In anger, he crushed
a wine glass, severing a tendon and finishing up in hospital. It was not a happy
period for Steve: he was in the process of divorcing his first wife Ellen Busse
and was disenchanted with the recording of *The Lamb* despite some exemplary
guitar contributions.

By contrast, recording *Voyage of the Acolyte* was an enjoyable, if challenging
experience. The four-week recording schedule in the summer of 1975 was
sandwiched between *The Lamb* tour and rehearsals for the *A Trick of the Tail*
album. Due to restrictions at Kingsway Studios, no music could be played
before 6 pm which resulted in a series of all-night recording sessions. However,
Steve had complete control and everyone involved seemed eager to make the
album a success. In addition to guitar, he plays several instruments including
Mellotron which he spent hours noodling on when writing the album. He also
co-produced the record, which set a precedent for his future work. Feeling that
the production style on the Genesis albums had become a little safe, he aimed
for a more powerful sound on tracks like 'A Tower Struck Down' and 'Shadow
of the Hierophant'.

Although Steve, Phil and Sally Oldfield sing on one song apiece, the majority
of the album demonstrates his flair for instrumentals. He experimented with
ideas that he felt Genesis would avoid but steered away from flashy guitar
soloing in favour of a wide spectrum of instrumental textures and colours that
had an orchestral quality. In contrast, he attempted a track with heavy chords in
the style of Pete Townshend based on the Fool tarot card, but it was abandoned
when he decided it sounded 'hammy'.

The album was positively received by the UK music press including *Melody
Maker* and *Sounds* who generally praised its lack of self-indulgence. For
some, it was a revelation and a telling indication of Steve's often undervalued
contribution to Genesis. On 1 November, it entered the UK chart at a
respectable 26 and remained in the top 50 for four weeks – not bad for a debut
solo album. The lacklustre showing in America and many other regions was a
foretaste of things to come. The evocative cover painting was by Brazilian artist
Kim Poor.

'Ace of Wands' 5:25 (Steve Hackett)

The Ace of Wands tarot card signifies new beginnings, creativity and a sense
of urgency, very appropriate for this strong opening statement. Steve wanted
to cram as much as he could into the track to grab the listener's attention.
A rousing instrumental, it has all the Genesis hallmarks although the pace is
more urgent than anything the band had attempted. Searing guitar and synth
exchanges are swept along by Collins and Rutherford's rapid-fire, but articulate,
rhythmic tide, the energy belying the fact that it recorded around three o'clock in

the morning. The bridge featuring double-tracked twelve-string guitars, heavenly Mellotron choir, flute and chiming tubular bells – shades of Mike Oldfield – at 0:58 and 2:12 is on a par with the best of Genesis' melodious moments.

The lengthy coda that kicks in at 3:23 features some of Steve's most exhilarating electric guitar runs. Tonally, the guitar is barely indistinguishable from John's rudimentary but effective ARP synth that shadows it. From his early days with Genesis, Steve has been fascinated by the potential of producing sounds that blur the distinction between guitar and keyboards. Following a false ending at 3:20, a new melody is introduced and as they power headlong to the finish, it's almost a race to see who can get there first. By my estimation, Steve wins by a nose.

'Hands of the Priestess, Part I' 3:29 (Hackett)

In tarot card meanings, the High Priestess represents intuition, mystery, sensuality and common sense. Chimes and rippling twelve-string on a bed of Mellotron strings set the tone for John's almost heartbreaking flute melody. Mournful, weeping electric guitar adds a hint of melancholy for one of Steve's most understated and exquisite instrumentals.

'Hands of the Priestess' was the first track recorded for the album. Pleased with the results, it gave Steve the confidence to record the other, more elaborately-arranged tracks. He didn't intend this to be a straightforward guitar album; he wanted to act as a facilitator for the other instruments, creating a broad spectrum of sound. The track fades to make way for...

'A Tower Struck Down' 4:52 (Steve Hackett, John Hackett)

A monumental fuzz-bass riff and staccato guitar chords bring to mind Led Zeppelin's 'Kashmir' released on *Physical Graffiti* earlier that same year. The quirky guitar, synth and Mellotron bridge at 1:17 and 2:17, however, is pure King Crimson with a dash of Genesis circa *The Lamb Lies Down on Broadway*. Swirling synths are interspersed with sampled sounds including catcalls and 'Sieg Heil' chants before the tower comes crashing down. The final minute is given over to an eerie Mellotron and nylon guitar sequence.

The Tower tarot card represents chaos and destruction. It's thought to be based on God's destruction of the Tower of Babel as told in the Bible, which also seems to be the impetus for Hackett's composition. The Nazi salute provides a more contemporary setting, however. In 1975 the atrocities of the second world war from 30 years earlier were still vivid in the memories of those that had lived through it. Like 'Ace of Wands', this track was performed on the 1978 *Please Don't Touch!* Tour and was destined to become a live favourite.

'Hands of the Priestess, Part II' 1:35 (Hackett)

Out of the ashes of 'A Tower Struck Down', cor anglais and flute reprise the theme from part one, unscored by acoustic rhythm and gorgeous electric guitar soloing.

'The Hermit' 4:49 (Hackett)

Closing side one of the original vinyl LP is the oldest song on the album, written five years earlier. It's the only vocal on side one, featuring Steve's first vocal outing on record. A brooding song, his voice is wisely measured and relatively low key, beneath a veil of acoustic guitar and cello with flute taking up the instrumental bridge. The melancholic lyrics reflect on the loneliness of old age, a perfect evocation of the Hermit tarot card which indicates a period of soul searching, self-reflection and potential spiritual enlightenment. The song's highpoint, however, is the instrumental second half beginning at 2:38. It features Robin Miller's sumptuous cor anglais solo that foreshadows the pastoral style of Anthony Phillips' debut album *The Geese & the Ghost* released eighteen months later.

'Star of Sirius' 7:08 (Hackett)

To open side two, Steve chose a pivotal song with an upbeat, almost pop sensibility to balance the album's heavier and the more introspective tracks. The lengthy intro, however, is on familiar ground with Phil Collins' mellow, double-tracked vocals accompanied by counterpoint acoustic guitars, Mellotron strings, discrete synth and vibes. It kicks up its heels at 3:25 for the memorable choral hook with Phil on drums and Roxy Music bassist John Gustafson proving to be a dynamic rhythm partnership. Robin Miller once again steals the show with a gorgeous oboe theme during the instrumental bridge at 3:42.

The Star tarot card indicates hope, inspiration and contentment, usually depicted by a naked woman kneeling by a pool of water. Steve also enters Sirius into the equation, the brightest star in the night sky for the chorus 'He who knows love knows who you are, Worlds you may find lit by a star'. This was Phil's third outing as a lead vocalist and the first to demonstrate he could carry an up-tempo song. Previously, he had been the singer of choice for tranquil offerings like Genesis' 'For Absent Friends' and 'More Fool Me' and Ant Phillips' yet to be released debut album. The *A Trick of the Tail* album which was just four months away would fully demonstrate his newfound vocal confidence.

'Star of Sirius' was performed on Steve's debut tour in the autumn of 1978 with his new vocal discovery Pete Hicks proving to be a worthy substitute for Collins. The band's accomplished performance can be viewed on *The Bremen Broadcast* DVD recorded on 8 November 1978.

'The Lovers' 1:49 (Hackett)

With the exception of the solo track 'Horizons' which introduced 'Supper's Ready' on the *Foxtrot* album and 'Blood on the Rooftops' on *Wind & Wuthering*, Steve had few opportunities to showcase his classical guitar talents within Genesis. Here, nylon guitar is joined by flute and what sounds like a backwards electric guitar for this lyrical, but all too short, instrumental that really deserved to be developed further. Unsurprisingly, the Lovers card represents harmony, love and attraction.

13

'Shadow of the Hierophant' 11:45 (Hackett, Mike Rutherford)

A song of two halves, this mini-epic was co-written with the Genesis bassist and originally rehearsed by the band during the 1972 *Foxtrot* sessions. Steve's attempts to get them to record it, however, were to no avail. It was first performed on his 1978 autumn tour and of all the tracks on *Voyage of the Acolyte*, it would prove to have the most staying power, remaining a live favourite to this day. The Hierophant tarot card signifies traditional values and convention and often features an image of the Pope.

The majestic – and very Genesis – intro of Mellotron, guitar swells and grandiose chords punctuate the otherwise haunting opening song section. Acoustic twelve-string and flute, back Sally Oldfield's ethereal vocals which contain evocative lines like 'Tears fill the fountains breaking their promise to heal'. Until this recording, Sally had been best known for her work with brother Mike. The instrumental bridge at 4:40 is pure Hackett featuring his trademark guitar tapping and a soaring theme which subsides at 5:54 to make way for the extended coda.

Over the course of almost six minutes, the instrumental finale builds from gentle beginnings in a similar fashion to ELP's 'Abaddon's Bolero' and the finale to part one of Mike Oldfield's *Tubular Bells*. Following a short xylophone solo, the instrumentation becomes denser as the volume gradually increases, driven by Collins' syncopated rhythms. Despite the arrival of tubular bells, the expected climax doesn't arrive and there is a slow fade instead. Steve clearly put everything into this tour de force and technically it remains one of his most ambitious pieces, capturing the power and majesty for which he was striving at the time. As kit drums do not feature throughout the track, a click track was used to keep time which, at that point, was a new experience for Collins.

Related Tracks

A CD remaster of *Voyage of the Acolyte* was released in September 2005 by Charisma/Virgin Records with two bonus tracks.

'Ace of Wands' (Live) 6:32 (Hackett)

This live version was recorded at London's Theatre Royal, Drury Lane on 11 November 1979 during the *Spectral Mornings* tour. Although the audio is a little compressed, the band is in fine fettle. Led by drummer John Shearer's storming intro, they're off the starting blocks like a speeding train with John Hackett, bassist Dik Cadbury and keyboardist Nick Magnus perfectly capturing the essence of the original. The barnstorming finale is absent, however, which was often played at the end of 'Racing in A'. It's replaced by a tranquil interlude with Steve indulging in seagull and whale-like guitar effects, which accounts for the track's extended length.

'Shadow of the Hierophant' (Extended Playout Version) 17:00
(Hackett, Rutherford)

Although this adds over five minutes to the album's original closing track, it doesn't improve it. The build during the extended finale now sounds a tad laboured. Rutherford's bass is more prominent in the mix, although at the expense of other instruments like the tubular bells. As before, it's Collins' explosive drum fills that provide the momentum.

Please Don't Touch! (1978)

Personnel:
Steve Hackett: electric guitar, acoustic guitar, Roland GR-500 guitar synthesiser; vocals on 'Carry On Up the Vicarage', backing vocals, keyboards, percussion
John Hackett: flute, piccolo, bass pedals, keyboards
Tom Fowler: bass
Chester Thompson: drums, percussion
John Acock: keyboards
Additional personnel:
Steve Walsh: lead vocals on 'Narnia, 'Racing in A'
Richie Havens: lead vocals on 'How Can I?', 'Icarus Ascending', percussion
Randy Crawford: lead vocals on 'Hoping Love Will Last'
Phil Ehart: drums, percussion on 'Narnia', 'Racing in A'
Dave Lebolt: keyboards
Hugh Malloy: cello
Graham Smith: violin
James Bradley: percussion
Maria Bonvino: female soprano on 'Hoping Love Will Last'
Feydor: vocals on 'The Voice of Necam'
Dan Owen: vocals on 'Icarus Ascending'
Dale Newman: vocals on 'Icarus Ascending'
Produced by John Acock, Steve Hackett
Engineered by John Acock
Recorded at: Kingsway Recorders, London; Cherokee Studios, Hollywood, California; Record Plant, Los Angeles; De Lane Lea Studios, Soho, London
Recording date: November 1977 – February 1978
Release date: May 1978
Record label: UK: Charisma Records, USA: Chrysalis Records
Highest chart places: UK: 38, USA: 103
Running time: 38:35

In the summer of 1977, during the mixing of the *Seconds Out* live album, Steve gave notice that he was quitting Genesis. Following the success of *Voyage of the Acolyte,* he had been writing an increasing number of songs and had argued that the *Wind & Wuthering* album should contain an equal share of his material. Unable to continue working within the constraints of a band co-operative and harbouring a desire for greater autonomy, Steve took his leave in October. He wanted to diversify, exploiting his guitar and songwriting talents to the full. He had also learnt a good deal about production from the first album and wanted to experiment with his own ideas.

He immediately set about recording his second album. Some of the songs included had been intended for Genesis while others were written specifically for the album. As was common practice for Steve, the songs were mostly written on nylon guitar, but he took a more eclectic approach this time, combining the melodic, prog-rock style of the first album with a more radio-friendly, AOR sound. The tracks were generally more song-based and Steve spent six weeks or so recording in Los Angeles before returning to London to complete the album, while several guest singers from America were engaged to give the album a transatlantic sound. He also attempted a more ethnic approach, hence the involvement of Richie Havens, Randy Crawford and Genesis touring drummer Chester Thompson. According to Steve, UK label Charisma and US label Chrysalis had differing views on the kind of artist he should be, which coloured the way the album turned out. He later reflected that: 'the 'European' styled tracks came more naturally to me'.

For Steve, it was an anxious time. While he believed leaving Genesis was artistically the right decision, from a commercial viewpoint, he was concerned. Although the album received positive reviews and spent five weeks in the UK top 50, he was conscious of the need to assemble a band to promote both *Please Don't Touch!* and *Voyage of the Acolyte*. This was a challenge as none of the singers on either of the albums were available, but by the end of August 1978, he had assembled his band. In addition to material from the first two albums, new songs destined for *Spectral Mornings* were rehearsed along with the Genesis standard, 'I Know What I Like (In Your Wardrobe)'. Opening at Chateau Neuf in Oslo, Norway on 4 October and closing at London's Hammersmith Odeon on 30 October, the European and UK tour was a resounding success. Although he gave a lot of credit to the new band, it was a vital boost to Steve's confidence as a solo artist.

Kim Poor's cover painting is a departure from her usual style. It depicts an elderly couple being attacked by mechanical toys within a Victorian fairground style frame, influenced by the track 'Carry On Up the Vicarage'. The reverse side features a moody, sepia-tinged photo of Steve with Brighton pier in the background.

'Narnia' 4:07 (Steve Hackett)

While Steve was writing the album, American prog-rockers Kansas had had a radio hit with 'Carry On Wayward Son' and he was impressed by the big, acapella vocals on the track. The band cited Genesis as an influence and Steve invited Kansas singer Steve Walsh and drummer Phil Ehart to perform on two songs. Given that the subject – the children's classic *The Lion, the Witch and the Wardrobe* – is a very British one, the distinctively American vocals and the song are ill-matched. The song's jaunty, upbeat tone also overlooks the dark humour and foreboding atmosphere of C.S. Lewis' novel.

That said, it's a suitably lively opener with chiming, double-tracked acoustic guitars joined by honky-tonk piano and Walsh's exuberant vocals. Ehart and bassist Tom Fowler make the most of the basic rhythm, with the latter's fluid playing in particular impressing. Steve's electric guitar, on the other hand, is mostly relegated to providing fills. Unsurprisingly, 'Narnia' was performed on the subsequent tour. Although Pete Hicks was relatively unknown as a frontman, it was the similarity between his voice and Walsh's that earned him a place in Steve's band three months after the album's release.

'Carry On Up the Vicarage' 3:11 (Hackett)

Another track with a very British subject matter, this is a homage to crime novelist Agatha Christie with a nod to the farcical 'Carry On' films popular during the 1960s and early '70s. The song is rife with lines that could have come straight from Christie's books. It opens with the sound of a children's musical box and part of a vintage recording of the Christmas carol 'Deck the Halls'. Chiming, Christmassy percussion ushers in a mighty organ combined with a touch of distorted guitar. The Robert Morgan pipe organ recorded at the Record Plant in Los Angeles, features on this track but not long after, it was sadly destroyed in a fire at the studio.

This is Steve's second vocal outing – following 'The Hermit' on the previous album. His double-tracked voice is heavily distorted to create the effect of a deep-voiced man and a squeaky-voiced child singing in unison. It's disconcerting, but it's all part of the song's quirky – if slightly sinister – charm. For the bridge beginning at 2:02, he sings in his normal pitch, although his voice remains processed.

'Racing in A' 5:07 (Hackett)

This is an aptly titled song – it is in the key of A – and it motors along at a breathless pace with Walsh's energetic vocals to the fore. As is typical of several Hackett songs from this period including 'Shadow of the Hierophant' and 'Every Day', it's in two distinct parts. His time with Genesis had clearly stood him in good stead when it came to combining sections of music. Compared with 'Narnia', the song's mood is more in keeping with the lyrics which soundly advise that we should get away from the pressures of life and take a break in the warm country air. It also has a better melody. Walsh was uncomfortable with Steve's original words and although uncredited, he rewrote them to suit his vocal style better.

The storming, single chord intro is superb, with Steve, Ehart and Fowler gelling as if they've been playing together for years. Steve's tricky, siren-like guitar line which punctuates each chorus is especially memorable. At 3:52, the song takes an unexpected turn with a nylon guitar solo providing a tranquil respite to the bombast that has preceded it. When performed live, this section, for obvious reasons, was jettisoned and the band would usually segue into the closing part of 'Ace of Wands' instead.

'Kim' 2:14 (Hackett)

This graceful, acoustic instrumental continues in a similar vein to the closing part of the previous track. It's more gentle and reflective, however. The lilting melody and slow, stop-start rhythm with Steve's nylon guitar accompanied by John's flute is clearly a homage to Erik Satie's exquisite tone poem

'Gymnopédie No 1'. The French composer and this piece, in particular, is greatly admired by both Hackett brothers and in 2000 they would release the *Sketches of Satie* tribute album. 'Kim' became a substantial live favourite and was often performed as a medley during the acoustic part of the show. It was reinterpreted by Steve and John on the 1983 classical album *Bay of Kings* with keyboardist Nick Magnus adding orchestral embellishments.

'How Can I?' 4:35 (Hackett)

After recording his vocals for 'Icarus Ascending' on side two, American folk and blues legend Richie Havens assisted Steve in finalising the song which closes side one, which lay half-finished. The opening voice at the Woodstock festival in 1969, he was the opening act when Genesis played three sell-out nights at London's Earls Court in 1977 shortly before Steve's departure. The pair developed a friendship and Steve suggested that they should later work together.

The song has a mellow, folky vibe with Steve's strummed twelve-string acoustic chords accompanying Havens' unmistakably warm and husky delivery. He flew from New York to Los Angeles specifically to record his vocals. A touch of harmonium and tambourine are the only other ingredients needed. Indeed, the melancholic lyrics are some of Steve's most mature and could have been penned by Havens himself. They tell of a man down on his luck whose partner has seemingly walked out on him. This was the only single release from the album – with 'Kim' as the B side. While it's a song of high quality, it doesn't exactly smack of hit potential and failed to chart despite the intimate promo video filmed near London's Kensington Gardens by famed director Tony Palmer.

'Hoping Love Will Last' 4:21 (Hackett)

This is Steve's most romantic and commercial sounding song thus far on the album, so why it wasn't released as a single is difficult to fathom. American jazz and R&B singer Randy Crawford was relatively unknown at the time with her big hit 'One Day I'll Fly Away' still two years away. She also sang lead vocals on the Crusader's 1979 jazz-funk anthem 'Street Life'. Steve spotted Randy singing in a Chicago club and she was an inspired choice for this sumptuous ballad. The combination of her soulful voice and Steve's weeping guitar are a match made in heaven. He was heartened by the favourable reaction from his ex-bandmates when they heard this song; it might have been an ideal vehicle for Phil Collins had Steve remained in Genesis.

There's a touch of sadness and insecurity in the lyrics; a yearning plea for a loving relationship not to falter, perhaps reflecting Steve's own uncertainty about love at the time. Lines like 'How can I go on alone when your love is all I've known' are some of his most direct and poetic and he even throws in a reference to William Shakespeare for good measure. The orchestral sequence at 2:26 is heavenly and when Randy's voice re-enters at 3:00 – sounding not unlike Aretha Franklin – it's simply stunning. Another American singer, Maria

Bonvino, is credited as 'guest female soprano' on the sleeve notes although her contribution is hard to spot.

'Land of a Thousand Autumns' 1:44 (Hackett)

Steve is on more familiar, proggy ground with this atmospheric instrumental which, like all the tracks on side two, blends seamlessly with the previous one. It serves as an introduction to the title track with the rich tones of the Roland GR-500 guitar synthesiser bookending rippling twelve-string chords and recorded crow caws.

'Please Don't Touch' 3:39 (Hackett)

Chester Thompson's explosive drum volley announces the title track in style. It's a gutsy instrumental with tricky time signatures, a throbbing bassline underpinning guitar, the GR-500, synth and electric piano. The bridge at 1:36 in 5/4 time with Steve's nimble guitar shadowed by John's equally dexterous flute is a delight, influenced by Dave Brubeck's jazz standard 'Take Five'. Along with 'Narnia', 'Carry On Up the Vicarage', 'Kim', 'Racing in A' and 'Icarus Ascending', it unsurprisingly found its way into the setlist of the 1978 tour and in terms of live performance, it's the album track that's best endured the test of time.

'Please Don't Touch' was a contender for Genesis' *Wind & Wuthering* album and although rehearsed, it was rejected in favour of Phil Collins' instrumental 'Wot Gorilla?' Steve felt very strongly about his track and clearly, the rest of the band's rejection of it played a part in his decision to quit the band. He even received an additional writing credit on 'Unquiet Slumbers for the Sleepers....' to placate him. According to Steve, after hearing this version, Phil later told him that he wished Genesis had recorded it. Steve later adapted the theme for the track 'Hackett to Bits', his solo contribution to the 1986 *GTR* album. Thanks to Geoff Downes overly bright production, his guitar tone on that version is very different from the one here, bringing to mind Yes-West's Trevor Rabin.

'The Voice of Necam' 3:11 (Hackett)

In the album's sleeve notes, the credits state 'Also starring Necam – The Computer' which, as the title suggests, comes into its own on this track. The mixing console at London's De Lane Lea Studios incorporated the Necam system of automated moving faders and although it produced clean, hiss free sounds, it proved to be troublesome at times. It opens with the jaunty sound of the Robert Morgan pipe organ before a dense, shimmering vocal loop rises – sun-like – over the horizon. The effect, combining several different voices, is stunning and is clearly influenced by 10cc's groundbreaking 1975 UK chart-topper 'I'm Not in Love'. The classical guitar melody that begins at 1:50, however, is all Steve and is one of his loveliest and most understated.

'Icarus Ascending' 6:20 (Hackett)

For the album's closing – and longest – track, Steve turns to one of his favourite subjects, Greek mythology. It's the late Richie Havens' second vocal contribution although it was recorded in 1977 before 'How Can I?' on side one. In many ways it's a stronger offering with Havens' emotive singing perfectly underscored by Steve's jangly rhythm, wailing lead fills and the rich chordal vocals from the previous track. The chorus is particularly memorable and only the disjointed instrumental bridge at 2:10 seems out of place. A short burst of reggae guitar and a dance band interlude are just two of the anomalies before the song regains its composure at 3:03. The extended playout at 3:42 is superb with Havens' soulful wordless vocals supported by buoyant flute and piano with Chester Thompson and Tom Fowler propelling the song to its slow fade.

'Icarus Ascending' has enjoyed a new lease of life in recent years and was performed as recently as 2018 with a fine vocal from Phil Collins soundalike Nad Sylvan. Havens himself later recorded with Peter Gabriel before his death in 2013 at the age of 72.

Related Tracks

The Charisma/Virgin Records 2005 CD remaster contains three bonus tracks. Like all of Steve's reissues in this period, the album was remastered by Benedict Fenner who has worked with Steve as an engineer, musician and co-songwriter for many years.

'Narnia' (John Perry Vocal Version) 3:36 (Hackett)

The original album version of 'Narnia' with Steve Walsh on vocals received plenty of airplay on American FM radio and Chrysalis wanted to release it as a single. Kansas' record company Epic objected, so this alternate version featuring musician and songwriter John Perry was prepared, but unfortunately Charisma didn't feel it was strong enough for release. Musically, it's identical to the original – albeit half a minute shorter thanks to a fade before the acoustic guitar and whistling coda. While Perry's singing doesn't have the same charismatic presence as Walsh, he still does a credible job.

'Land of a Thousand Autumns/Please Don't Touch' (Live) 7:53 (Hackett)

This is a stunning live version of this album pairing. The powerhouse rhythm section of bassist Dik Cadbury and drummer John Shearer make it their own and Steve tears the piece apart with his guitar histrionics. The superb recording and remastering also ensure that John's flute maintains its presence and is not buried beneath the sheer weight of the other instrumentation.

The sleeve notes on the 2005 reissue incorrectly list the playing time as 1:44. It also gives no indication of when and where it was recorded, but I'm assuming it was on the 1978 or 1979 tour. There's an extended version on the

2CD *Cured In Cleveland* recorded for FM radio on 20 October 1981. Although it's an unofficial release and sound quality is not on a par with this version, it's still a must-listen.

'Narnia' (Alternate Version) 4:31 (Hackett)

An extended version of the original opening track with Steve Walsh on vocals. The recorded sounds of children playing at the end of the original is replaced with an acoustic guitar loop and Steve's processed harmonies that continue for around half a minute.

'Seven of Cups' 3:32 (Hackett)

A previously unreleased bonus track on the 2015 box-set *Promotions: The Charisma Recordings 1975-1983*. Recorded in 1978 during the *Please Don't Touch!* sessions, it's a piano-driven instrumental with a smooth jazz flavour, sounding very un-Hackett like. In addition to the impressively fluid piano playing, the articulate drumming stands out with engaging flute and acoustic guitar embellishments. The rhythmic acoustic guitar part at the 1:43 mark would be reused in 'The Virgin and the Gypsy' on the *Spectral Mornings* album.

Spectral Mornings (1979)

Personnel:
Steve Hackett: electric and acoustic guitars, Roland GR-500 guitar synthesiser; lead vocals, harmonica on 'The Ballad of the Decomposing Man'; harmony/backing vocals on 'Every Day', 'The Virgin and the Gypsy'; koto on 'The Red Flowers of Tachai Blooms Everywhere'
Pete Hicks: lead vocals on 'Every Day', 'The Virgin and the Gypsy', 'Tigermoth'
Dik Cadbury: bass guitar; harmony/backing vocals on 'Every Day', 'The Virgin and the Gypsy', 'Tigermoth'; Moog Taurus bass pedals, violin on 'The Ballad of the Decomposing Man'
Nick Magnus: keyboards, Vox String Thing, Novatron, clavinet, Fender Rhodes & RMI electric pianos, Minimoog, Mini-Korg 700, Roland String Synth RS-202 & SH-2000; harpsichord on 'The Virgin and the Gypsy'
John Hackett: flute, bamboo flute on 'The Virgin and the Gypsy'; Moog Taurus bass pedals on 'Clocks – The Angel of Mons'
John Shearer: drums, percussion
Produced by John Acock, Steve Hackett
Recorded at: Phonogram Studios, Hilversum, the Netherlands
Recording date: January – February 1979
Release date: 26 May, 1979
Record label: UK: Charisma Records, USA: Chrysalis Records
Highest chart places: UK: 22, USA: 138
Running time: 39:03

Buoyed with the success of the 1978 tour, Steve entered Phonogram's Wisseloord Studios in Hilversum at the start of the new year to begin work on his third album. This time, rather than a succession of guests, he took his touring band with him who had developed into a versatile unit. Indeed, the desire to be able to perform the music live influenced his approach to the album. The studio was huge and had been open for just twelve months, boasting state of the art facilities. It was the middle of winter, snow lay deep and the nearby lake was frozen over so apart from the occasional bouts of partying, there was little to distract from the intense sessions which continued day and night.

Steve was totally immersed in the album and specific themes began to develop, including references to the first world war and also death. He was a member of the Spiritualist Association of Great Britain at the time and as a result, his research inspired the songs 'Clocks – The Angel of Mons' and 'Tigermoth'. On stage, Pete Hicks had proven himself to be a more than capable frontman and sang most of the lead vocals, assisted by vocal contributions from bassist Dik Cadbury and Steve himself. Indeed, Cadbury, a classically trained singer and ex-member of prog-folk pioneers Decameron, arranged the harmonies. Overall, however, this was a return to the instrumental opulence of *Voyage of the Acolyte*. Versatile keyboardist Nick

Magnus had performed with The Enid in the past while drummer John Shearer – armed with his imposing 24-piece stainless steel kit – was formerly with Quiver. While the songs on *Please Don't Touch!* had been tailored to suit the individual singers, here Steve's musical ambitions were given free rein without restrictions.

Steve was particularly proud of the finished results, feeling that it contained his best work and best playing thus far. Charisma label boss Tony Stratton-Smith was equally impressed. Critics and record buyers generally agreed, it was his highest-charting album yet and spent almost three months in the UK top 75. For many fans, it's Steve's best album and several songs remain in his setlist to this day. The opening song 'Every Day', 'Clocks' and the closing instrumental are undoubtedly his signature pieces.

Following the recording, Steve and the band took to the road once more, touring Europe and the UK throughout most of 1979. This included a triumphant appearance at the Reading Festival on Saturday 25 August, while ex-bandmate Peter Gabriel headlined the following day. With three albums to select from, the setlist for this tour was more varied, although the perennial 'I Know What I Like (In Your Wardrobe)' was once again included in the encore. Indeed, while taking the music seriously, the band had grown in confidence and were not opposed to having fun on stage, with Steve later remarking that the tour was a joy.

The cover artwork echoes the album's theme. Steve's pale visage, with eyes half-closed, appears almost ghost-like through the airbrushed mist. His photo on the reverse in his now-familiar Regency-style, gipsy stagewear was taken from a filmed recording for German TV on 8 November 1978.

'Every Day' 6:15 (Steve Hackett)

Album openers do not come much better than this. A song of two halves, the first section features a sunny chorus with three-part harmonies and a sprightly instrumental hook belying the dark subject matter. An anti-drugs statement, it relates to Steve's first girlfriend who became an addict, underlined by the chilling line 'You became a ghost to me long before you died'. It serves as a prelude to the barnstorming instrumental coda, heralded by a stunning, ringing guitar fanfare at 3:10.

The three minute solo on his customised – and double-tracked – Les Paul, incorporates several Hackett trademark innovations including finger vibrato and a sustained, tremolo-arm 'dive bomb' at 5:33. It's his best solo since the instrumental bridge during Genesis' 'Firth of Fifth' although there were – arguably – better to come. John Shearer recalled that they trialed the newly-developed Simmons electronic drums on this track, but they were deemed too 'disco' sounding for the album. The distinctive 'boing' at 1:08 was produced by a drum synth.

'Every Day' became an instant stage favourite and remains Steve's most played non-Genesis song. Although the tempo has speeded-up a little over the years and he adds different nuances to the solo, it's always played to perfection. Without the fade that mars the studio version, the intro is usually reprised to end the song on a dramatic note. A drastically edited 2:41 version was the first single released from the album in June 1979.

'The Virgin and the Gypsy' 4:29 (Hackett)

When Steve wrote this song, he hadn't actually read D. H. Lawrence's 1926 novel based around a post-world war one romance, but he liked the title. It also remains one of his favourite songs on the album. It's a beautiful evocation of rural England on a summer's day with references to wildflowers including Milk Thistle, Ragged-Robin and Sweet Marigold. The idea came from *A Victorian Book of Flowers,* which Steve was reading at the time along with, as he put it, 'A couple of glasses of wine'. Twelve-string guitar, harpsichord, double-tracked flutes and guitar synth combine to create, in his own words 'the effect of a colliery brass band twinned with accordion'.

The lush three-part harmonies are superb, creating a vocal opulence in keeping with the lyrical imagery. Despite the pastoral ambience, the Roland GR-500 sounds completely appropriate, especially during the otherwise-acoustic instrumental sequence. Not surprisingly, drums and bass are absent.

'The Red Flower of Tachai Blooms Everywhere' 2:05 (Hackett)

This is a compact but sumptuous instrumental for Mellotron fans. In keeping with the evocative title, it's a gorgeous aural tapestry with a distinctly oriental flavour. Opening with a short solo played on Cantonese koto, the listener is transported on a sea of strings, conjuring up romantic images of the far east. In addition to the koto, discrete percussion and Chinese bamboo flute add to the atmosphere.

Surprisingly, this delicate, multi-tracked instrumental transferred successfully to the stage, thanks to the consummate skill of Steve and his band. When I saw them perform this in 1979, it sounded every bit as good as the studio version. It segues into...

'Clocks – The Angel of Mons' 4:17 (Hackett)

We go from the sublime to the downright bombastic. A mighty and menacing instrumental, 'Clocks' was performed on the 1978 *Please Don't Touch!* tour prior to this recording. Shearer's experimentations with tribal drum sounds formed the basis of the track. Pink Floyd famously recorded real clocks for *The Dark Side of the Moon* track 'Time', but here, Steve recreates the 'tick-tock' sound by ingenious manipulation of the guitar strings using a pick. The rhythmic, scraping sound at 2:13 is produced by sliding his right hand rapidly up and down the full length of the strings. The ominous sound of Mellotron strings and bass pedals – rarely sounding as powerful as they do here – demonstrates a specific Genesis influence. The pedals go an octave lower than a bass guitar and are played by John Hackett using his hands rather than his feet. All hell breaks loose with the drum solo at 3:06.

The track – or at least the title – is based on a popular myth from the early part of the first world war. During the 1914 Battle of Mons, British troops, outnumbered by the advancing Germans, were supposedly protected by guardian angels. The 'Clocks' part is perhaps a reference to the bell tower that still dominates the Mons skyline, despite the city's devastation during two world wars. On stage, 'Clocks' took on a life of its own and became a showcase for Shearer's energetic drum talents. It left him physically drained after every performance and was nicknamed 'Elephants' because it sounded like a one-man stampede! It's regularly performed live and was the encore for the 2009-2010 *Out of the Tunnel's Mouth* tours.

'The Ballad of the Decomposing Man (featuring 'The Office Party')' 3:49 (Hackett)

During the 1970s, industrial relations in the UK were strained, resulting in mass strikes, power cuts and a three-day working week. This is a tongue-in-cheek parody of the stereotypical lifestyle and attitudes of the British working class and was perceived to be an anti-union song at the time, which Steve denied. Like 'Carry On Up the Vicarage' on the previous album and 'Sentimental Institution' on *Defector,* it was a not altogether successful attempt to add an element of humour to the album.

Following a *Sparky's Magic Piano* type processed voice intro – à la ELO's 'Mr Blue Sky'- Steve sings in a mock-Lancashire accent in the style of 1940's British musical hall star George Formby. Jaunty, bar-room piano and rat-a-tat percussion provide the backing and Steve plays a bluesy harmonica solo – his first on record – at 0:50. Guitar synth provides a brief moment of majesty before the song morphs into the 'The Office Party' at 2:02. This section has a distinct west-Indian flavour, complete with the sound of steel drums, in addition to Cadbury's Caribbean-flavoured bass pedals and Nick Magnus' calypso-style synth melody.

'Lost Time in Córdoba' 4:04 (Hackett)

To open side two of the vinyl LP, a serene, mostly acoustic piece featuring Steve on classical guitar, John on concert flute and Magnus on synth. During one of Steve's many travels, he visited the historic city of Córdoba in the Andalusia region of southern Spain which clearly left an intense impression. In the first part of the piece, a gentle nylon guitar melody is doubled by a flute. However, at 0:46, a solo guitar plays a different theme with repeated lines creating a haunting effect. Discrete synth – a Mini-Korg, in all likelihood – enters at 2:04 playing a different melody over Steve's rhythmic chords. A solo guitar plays out over the final 40 seconds. This piece is a foretaste of the mostly-acoustic 1983 *Bay of Kings* album and the 'acoustic trio' tours Steve later staged. It was released as the B-side to the 'Every Day' single in 1979.

'Tigermoth' 7:35 (Hackett)

The album's penultimate – and longest – track, is a ghost story that's almost cinematic in its scope. It opens with an instrumental sequence featuring ominous – and very King Crimson-sounding – bass and guitar with piercing, staccato chords creating a nightmarish effect. In contrast, the ethereal guitar synth theme is hauntingly beautiful. Steve was experimenting with different textures and liked the Roland GR-500's potential to create ambiguous, keyboard-like sounds. The – synthetically produced – sounds of diving planes and machine-gun fire set the scene for the song section.

Accompanied by delicate acoustic guitar, flute and synth washes, Hick's vocals do not enter until the four-minute mark and relate the death of an RAF pilot during the first world war. Following a fatal plane crash, he is reunited with his deceased comrades. Perhaps it's due to the slow, waltz-like lilt, but this song section is less convincing and it's almost an anticlimax compared with the instrumental sequence. The chorus of the song is underpinned by a military drum pattern, and the ethereal, rising harmonies at the end of the chorus evoke vintage Genesis. At 6:12, Steve brings the track to a serene conclusion with chiming, double-tracked twelve-string and six-string acoustic guitars.

'Spectral Mornings' 6:33 (Hackett)

The title track is the album's pièce de résistance and sums up the tone of the album beautifully. Following the overall theme of the previous song, for Steve, the title refers to a meditation on the afterlife and the release of the spirit following death. Inspired by the wintery recording location, he wanted the tranquil opening section to create an image of curtains opening to a snowy morning day. Shearer's bell tree glissando signals the opening of the curtains joined by the shimmering, choir-like wordless voices from 'The Voice of Necam' on *Please Don't Touch!*. The tranquil mood is broken by Steve's stunning guitar melody which soars into view at 0:55 on a wave of shimmering strings courtesy of Magnus' Vox String Thing. The chords and the ascending bass line reveal Bach's influence on Steve's writing.

It isn't just the melody and the quality of Steve's playing that makes this instrumental so compelling, the guitar's bright, searing tone is addictive. Prior to recording, it was performed on the 1978 tour and remains one of Steve's most played and best-loved pieces. When performed during the subsequent 1979 tour, John Hackett as the second guitarist played the arpeggio chords Steve plays on the album. 'Spectral Mornings' was a beacon of light for the neo-prog movement of the 1980s, inspiring many guitarists like Steve Rothery (Marillion), Nick Barrett (Pendragon) and Mike Holmes (IQ).

This was the first track recorded for the album and Steve originally envisaged 'Spectral Mornings' as a song, but when he played Hicks the melody, the singer convinced him to keep it as an instrumental. It did eventually appear in that form when it was re-recorded as 'Spectral Mornings 2015' with vocals and lyrics by David Longdon of Big Big Train. It was produced by Rob Reed of Welsh progressive rock band Magenta and the band's singer Christina Booth shared vocal duties with Longdon. Steve plays classical and lead guitar on the reworked track.

Related Tracks
The remastered CD released in 2005 by Virgin Records features seven bonus tracks. The track timings printed in the CD booklet are incorrect, those shown below are the correct track lengths.

'Every Day' (Alternate Mix) 7:10 (Hackett)
Hick's vocals during the chorus and the secondary guitar parts are brighter in the mix. Bass is more prominent in the instrumental sequence, which features a slow, extended playout.

'The Virgin and the Gypsy' (Alternate Mix) 4:29 (Hackett)
There's very little to distinguish this from the original, although the guitar synth is a tad more fulsome.

'Tigermoth' (Alternate Mix) 3:19 (Hackett)
This begins four minutes into the original track at the start of the song section. Dik Cadbury's falsetto vocals are more prominent during the chorus, more so than Hicks. The acoustic guitar coda also fades sooner.

'The Ballad of the Decomposing Man' (Alternate Mix) 4:23 (Hackett)
The overall sound is brighter and it features a more prominent banjo-like guitar during the first section. During 'The Office Party' sequence, the steel drum sound is not as full and female backing voices have more presence with an extended playout before the fade.

'Clocks – The Angel of Mons' (12" Single Version) 3:37 (Hackett)
This is an edited version released as the second single from the album in September 1979. It maintains the impact of the original, even though Shearer's drum solo at the end has around half a minute removed from it.

'Live Acoustic Set' 5:40 (Matteo Carcassi, Hackett, Phil Collins)
A beautifully performed acoustic set recorded on the *Spectral Mornings* tour. Steve performs a solo nylon guitar medley of Carcassi's 'Etude in A Minor' – arranged by Steve and John, plus a brief snippet of 'Blood on the Rooftops' and 'Horizons'. Following an enthusiastic response from the appreciative French crowd, he is joined by John's flute for a faithful rendition of 'Kim'. It was

recorded on 11 June 1979 at the Pavillon de Paris and was originally released as the B-side to the 'Clocks' twelve-inch single.

'Tigermoth' (Live Version) 3:58 (Hackett)
The second B-side to the 'Clocks' single, this was also recorded in Paris in June 1979. Purely instrumental, it forsakes the studio version's song section but is none the worse for that. The arrangement is also different with arguably more impact, alternating the heavier, bombastic parts with quiet, semi-improvised interludes.

'The Caretaker' (unlisted) 1:41 (Pete Hicks)
This is a hidden – and very funny – track at the end of the 2005 CD. There's no music; it's just Hicks – with a severe cough and a case of bad language – playing the part of a grumpy studio cleaner who has the unenviable task of clearing up after the band.

Defector (1980)

Personnel:
Steve Hackett: electric and acoustic guitars, Roland GR-500 guitar synthesiser; harmony vocals on 'Time to Get Out', 'The Toast'; Optigan on 'Sentimental Institution'
Pete Hicks: lead vocals on 'Time to Get Out', 'Leaving', 'The Toast', 'The Show', 'Sentimental Institution'
Dik Cadbury: bass guitar, Moog Taurus bass pedals; harmony/backing vocals on 'Time to Get Out', 'Leaving', 'The Toast', 'The Show'
Nick Magnus: keyboards, Prophet 5, Clavinet, Fender Rhodes & RMI electric pianos, Novatron, Vox String Thing, Minimoog, Roland SH-2000; Roland VP-330 vocoder on 'Slogans'; piano on 'Hammer in the Sand'
John Hackett: concert and alto flute
John Shearer: drums, percussion
Produced by: John Acock, Steve Hackett
Engineered by John Acock
Recorded at: Wessex Sound Studios, Highbury New Park, London
Recording date: Spring 1980
Release date: 21 June, 1980
Record label: Charisma Records
Highest chart places: UK: 9, USA: 144
Running time: 36:52

Defector is the last in the quartet of classic, early period Hackett albums. He retained the *Spectral Mornings* band for the recording, giving the two albums a unifying character. Compared with Hilversum, the sessions at Wessex Sound in London were more hurried and very workman-like. King Crimson had been a major influence on Steve and their debut album *In the Court of the Crimson King* had been recorded in the same studio eleven years earlier. A former church hall, the studio specialised in big, natural sounds. Additionally, unlike the previous albums, the sessions were squeezed between touring commitments and several songs were written during the rehearsals for the recording, although three songs – 'The Steppes', 'Sentimental Institution' and 'Hercules Unchained' – had already been road-tested during the November 1979 tour. Steve enjoyed the recording but wanted to finish as quickly as possible so that he and the band could get back out on the road, as he was still enjoying performing with his 'killer band'.

Although the album isn't a concept as such, it has a Cold War theme and Steve took inspiration from several sources including Bernardo Bertolucci's 1970 political film *The Conformist* and the 1966 thriller *Defector* starring Montgomery Clift. Indeed, during the late 1970s, several defectors from Eastern Europe to the west had made headline news, while the title is also symbolic of Steve's sudden departure from Genesis. In fact, some of the album was written in New York, where Steve sensed at first hand the uneasy alliance between America and Russia. Despite structural similarities between *Defector* and *Spectral Mornings*, this is generally a darker and heavier offering. For Steve, it contained some of his strongest instrumentals and songs that he had written up to that point and remains one of his personal favourites.

Soon after recording, the Steve Hackett band were back out on the road with a successful sell-out UK tour. The author was in the audience at the De Montfort Hall, Leicester on 23 June 1980 where Steve occupied centre-stage - with singer Pete Hicks positioned behind on a raised platform - producing a stunning show with three encores. On 14 June, *Defector* entered the UK chart at number sixteen and the following week it breached the top ten. Although it's not Steve's best selling album, it remains his highest-charting in the UK and lingered in the top 75 for seven weeks. In September and October, Steve played North America for the first time since Genesis' 1977 *Wind & Wuthering* tour – shortly before leaving the band – followed by more European dates in November.

The cover is almost a mirror image of *Spectral Mornings* although the deep red background is more in keeping with the theme of *Defector.*

'The Steppes' 6:04 (Steve Hackett)

Appropriately, the album's standout track opens proceedings. The title is a reference to the geographical area the Russian – AKA the Eurasian – Steppes and this instrumental evokes the landscape and the album's cold-war theme. It had been played as a stage number prior to the recording, under the unlikely working title of 'Eric'.

Following John Hackett's tranquil solo flute intro which evokes middle-eastern and Russian folk music, a drum volley announces a slow, relentless but magisterial march-like rhythm reminiscent of Ravel's 'Boléro'. A menacing guitar theme doubled by flute is backed by bass pedals and keyboard orchestrations. Indeed, the hypnotic, slow-burning effect hints at Weather Report's 'Scarlet Woman' from the 1974 *Mysterious Traveller* album. To create the powerful John Bonham-like stomp, John Shearer's drums were recorded in St Augustines Church in Highbury adjacent to Wessex Sound Studios. It acted as a natural echo chamber, giving the drums – played without cymbals – a booming resonance. Nick Magnus plays the newly developed Prophet Five synthesiser to simulate the brass sounds.

At exactly the halfway mark, the piece branches off into a stunning bridge section with lush Novatron strings and a full-blooded guitar melody before returning to the main theme. At 5:30, the track plays out with a lyrical, weeping guitar phrase. For Steve, this is the album's defining track and, understandably, became a stage favourite, opening the set on the *Highly Strung* tour in 1983. More recently, it has been resurrected for live performances with samples and reverb adding weight to the rhythm.

'Time to Get Out' 4:12 (Hackett)

A jaunty, swirling keyboard intro sets the scene for this cold war parody with sprightly three-part harmonies from Pete Hicks, Dik Cadbury and Steve. The upbeat, AOR style is reminiscent of the Steve Walsh songs on *Please Don't Touch!* The instrumental bridge at 1:52 sounds like it's beamed in from another song, but its memorable guitar and keyboard hook is a welcome intrusion. The wordless la-la-la vocal section at 2:31 feels a touch like padding before Steve plays out with a vibrant, finger tapping solo.

This is not one of the albums most inspired cuts in my view, although Cadbury's nimble bass playing is superb. Somehow, the song's tone doesn't quite match the subject – the cold war standoff between America and Russia and the 1960's Cuban Missile Crisis. Steve, however, considered it to be one of the strongest tunes he had written up to that point – along with 'Leaving', 'The Toast' and 'The Show'.

'Slogans' 3:58 (Hackett)

Although an instrumental, 'Slogans' is about propaganda and political rhetoric on both sides of the east-west and left-right divide. From the manic introduction to the symphonic finale, it's like 'Please Don't Touch' on acid. Built around Shearer's explosive drums, the piece goes through several, tricky time signatures. At 0:53, it boasts Steve's fastest guitar playing thus far and the guitar neck hammering – or tapping – is doubled-up by a Minimoog. When Magnus first joined Steve's band, he had a minimal keyboard set-up, but for this album, it had been greatly expanded. He uses a newly acquired Roland VP-330 Vocoder for the processed 'blah-blah-blah' vocals that accompany the main riff, reminiscent of Brian Eno's vocal effects on Genesis' *The Lamb Lies Down on Broadway.*

In between the mayhem, 'Slogans' is very Genesis-like at times with a Novatron providing the rich Mellotron-like string sounds. Cadbury's bass work is once again excellent and Shearer squeezes in a brief drum solo at 2:12. The closing synth-led theme at 3:10 really swings, curtailed by the descending string chords that bring the track to a peaceful conclusion. 'Slogans' was performed on both the *Defector* and *Cured* tours.

'Leaving' 3:04 (Hackett)

'Leaving' relates the ruminations of an exchanged defector and his culture shock of arriving in the west. It has a bleak, film noir quality that recalls the 1965 black and white cold-war spy film *The Spy Who Came In from the Cold* based on John le Carré's novel. The suitably subdued melody with chiming double-tracked twelve-string guitars and lush counterpoint harmonies is a throwback to 'The Virgin and the Gypsy' on the previous album. It has an added melancholia, however, with eerie synth washes and although there is no chorus as such, the Minimoog hook is simple but haunting. It is one of Steve's most understated, and shamefully overlooked songs.

'Two Vamps as Guests' 1:53 (Hackett)
Bringing side one of the vinyl LP full circle, we conclude with a solo nylon guitar piece that reprises the melody from 'The Steppes'. A beautiful, classically inspired variation on a theme, Steve's fingerpicking is a tasteful combination of skill and restraint.

'Jacuzzi' 4:37 (Hackett)
Side two opens with another stunning – although more upbeat – instrumental, that rivals 'The Steppes', 'Hammer in the Sand' and 'The Toast' as the album's best offering. Crackling with energy, the infectious, toe-tapping melody with ringing guitars, rippling flute and keyboard strings is sure to put a smile on the face of all but the most cynical listener. It hits a heavier stride at 1:28 with Steve's persistent guitar and Magnus' helter-skelter synth driven by Cadbury's funky bassline and Shearer's razor-sharp snare.

At 3:57, a new, but equally sprightly theme is introduced – which would have sat comfortably on the *Voyage of the Acolyte* – to bring the track to a satisfying close. On the subsequent *Defector* tour, 'Jacuzzi' was played as part of an impressive instrumental trio along with 'A Tower Struck Down' and 'Clocks'. Aside from 'Jacuzzi' being a euphemism for a hot tub – a symbol of western decadence – the title is perfect for this invigorating piece. After hearing it, in 1982 Keith Emerson asked Steve to form a band with him, Jack Bruce on bass and Simon Phillips on drums. Although some tapes were recorded over a three-day session, the band failed to come to fruition.

'Hammer in the Sand' 3:12 (Hackett)
Like 'Spectral Mornings' on the previous album, Steve originally conceived this as a song. The main studio at Wessex Sound housed a Bösendorfer grand piano and when Magnus sat down and played the melody unaccompanied, they both realised it would work better as an instrumental. Although a classically trained pianist, Magnus rarely played the instrument with Steve, but he certainly makes up for it here.

It begins with solo piano with Magnus tickling the ivories to rhapsodic effect, evoking the fluid, romantic style of Sergei Rachmaninoff. At 0:38, the hauntingly beautiful melody is enhanced by keyboard orchestrations with the analogue Prophet Five and the Novatron blending harmonically to produce a lush, symphonic backdrop. The Roland guitar synth theme at 1:18 is breathtaking, ebbing and flowing before the serene conclusion. It remains for me one of Steve's all-time best compositions and is one of his own personal favourites. Plans to re-record it one day with Magnus and a real orchestra remain unfulfilled.

The 'hammer' of the title is a reference to the might of Russia while 'sand' signifies the more benign aspect of the country's culture exemplified by the romantic music of Rachmaninoff. The fall of the Berlin Wall in November 1989 allowed for a different interpretation of the title. Like the hammer, the wall was a symbol of Russia's austerity and when it fell, it was reduced to sand and rubble.

'The Toast' 3:43 (Hackett)

Fueled by wine, the song's protagonist – portrayed by rich, three-part harmonies – reflects on the transience of love. He's backed by a mellow, twelve-string guitar melody that draws from the previous track. Like 'Kim' on *Please Don't Touch!*, the lilting keyboard string and flute bridge at 1:28 is indebted to Erik Satie's 'Gymnopédie No 1'. John's flute solo is exquisite with a bittersweet melody that's achingly beautiful. So much so, that when the otherwise engaging vocal melody returns at 3:00, it's almost an anticlimax. 'The Toast' was the B-side to the album's second single, 'Sentimental Institution', released in August 1980.

'The Show' 3:41 (Hackett)

Under pressure from Charisma Records to produce a hit single, 'The Show' was released in that format in March 1980 and although it received airplay in the UK, it failed to chart. Appropriately, the lyrics are a scathing comment on the money-driven aspects of the music business and the grind of life on the road. And if I'm not mistaken, the chorus is a veiled reference to attitudes towards The Beatles in the early 1960s.

Opening with a fat, disco-inspired bassline and early 1980s synth-pop keys, the contrast between this pop parody and 'The Toast' is jarring. Hicks enters into the spirit with an energetic lead vocal but the ponderous clump-clump, hand-clap rhythm doesn't really work. With Steve mostly playing ringing rhythm guitar, the short Prophet Five synth bridge at 2:11 is the song's best part. To reflect the song's theme of corporate rock, the 1980 promo video for the single shows Steve manipulating the band as faceless puppets dressed in business suits and bowler hats. I wonder if Charisma got the joke.

'Sentimental Institution' 2:40 (Hackett, Pete Hicks)

During the recording of Genesis' *Wind & Wuthering* album at Relight Studios in the Netherlands, Steve discovered an instrument called the Optigan. It had a keyboard and a facility to insert pre-recorded discs to produce specific sounds. Here, he uses it to create a pastiche of a 1940s big-band. To enhance the vintage feel, the track is treated to sound like an old 78 rpm gramophone record, complete with scratches. It was partly recorded in the men's toilets to add a touch of reverb and removing the top and bottom from the vocal created a megaphone style effect. Hicks really comes into his own, sounding like a 1940s crooner with a Satchmo impression thrown in for good measure. His in-joke lyrics reference American states and several famous jazz musicians from the period.

Along with 'The Steppes' and 'Hercules Unchained', 'Sentimental Institution' was written the previous year during a two-day band rehearsal. It worked surprisingly well live with the stage dressed and lit to resemble a vintage nightclub and Hicks dressed appropriately in a white dinner jacket. Like 'The Show', it was released as a single in 1980 and similarly failed to trouble the charts.

Related Tracks

The following are all bonus tracks on the 2005 CD reissue of *Defector,* remastered by Benedict Fenner. He also remastered the 2016 'Deluxe Edition' which includes a second CD recorded live at the annual Reading Festival on 28 August 1981. The 60-minute performance promoted the recently released *Cured* album and includes three songs from *Defector*, 'The Steppes', 'Slogans' and 'The Show'. A DVD is also included with a 'New pseudo 5.1 Surround Up-Mix from the original stereo master tapes'.

'Hercules Unchained' 2:44 (Hackett, Hicks)

Originally released in March 1980 as the B-side of 'The Show' single, this is a spoof punk-rock / power pop song – with a touch of speed-metal – and singer Hicks once again rises to the occasion. Although the title is borrowed from a 1959 Italian-French sword-and-sandal film, the angry lyrics relate to a violence obsessed protagonist and his uneasy relationships. It's convincingly executed and probably the most un-Hackett like song in Steve's vast canon.

'Sentimental Institution' 2:38 (Hackett, Hicks)

A live version from the *Spectral Mornings* tour, recorded at London's Theatre Royal, Drury Lane on 11 November 1979. It's barely disguisable from the studio version released seven months later showing that even at that stage, it had already been fully worked out as a song

'The Steppes' 6:33 (Hackett)

Along with the following two tracks, this was recorded live on 28 August 1981 at the Reading Festival in the south-east of England. It's meticulously performed – and recorded – perfectly recreating the majesty and power of the studio version. The drums – with added cymbal splashes – and bass pedals sound suitably weighty and Steve throws in a few extra guitar flourishes and effects for good measure. The performance is particularly impressive as this was one of the first performances to feature the new rhythm section of drummer Ian Mosley and bassist Chas Cronk.

'Slogans' 4:19 (Hackett)

Another instrumental skillfully performed live that does full justice to the original – although at a slightly faster pace. Steve's ultra-fast guitar gymnastics are jaw-droppingly impressive although Mosley's short drum solo sounds a tad clumsy compared with Shearer's original.

'Clocks – The Angel of Mons' 5:54 (Hackett)

Yet another version of this popular live workout, although it never fails to impress. This time, Mosley makes a better fist of his drum finale although he's almost drowned out by Magnus' 'wailing banshee' synth.

Cured (1981)

Personnel:
Steve Hackett: guitars, bass guitar, vocals
Nick Magnus: keyboards, LM-1 drum machine
Additional personnel:
John Hackett: flute on 'Overnight Sleeper', bass pedals on 'The Air-Conditioned Nightmare'
Bimbo Acock: saxophone on 'Picture Postcard'
Produced by: John Acock, Steve Hackett, Nick Magnus
Engineered by John Acock
Recorded at: Redan Studios, London
Recording date: Summer 1981
Release date: 14 August 1981
Record label: UK: Charisma Records, USA: Epic Records
Highest chart places: UK: 15, USA: 169
Running time: 33:51

Despite the success of the *Defector album* and tour, Steve found it financially impractical to maintain a full-time band while he was off the road and the 'killer' team was disbanded. Following the recording and heavy touring over the previous two years, he was mentally and physically drained and spent three months in Brazil writing and rethinking his recording strategy. The original plan was an acoustic album and half the material for that project was recorded before Steve took a more commercial direction.

Work began in earnest on *Cured* following his return to London. Despite fairly minimal singing experience, he took on all the vocals, utilising multi-tracking to create three-part harmonies. Nick Magnus was retained for both his keyboard talents and programming abilities – this was the age of the drum machine, a technology that he and Steve fully embraced. With John Acock co-producing his fifth Hackett album, it's mostly the work of the three men, although Steve's brother John features on two tracks and Bimbo Acock on one. The album title is a tongue-in-cheek reference to Steve's revitalised state following his recuperation in Brazil.

It's not only the leaner line-up that distinguishes *Cured* from its predecessors. While the previous albums had remained true to the prog-rock genre familiar to Genesis fans, this was in a very different style, being Americanised, early 1980s mainstream pop-rock. Under pressure from Charisma, Steve was attempting to create songs that would appeal to the American singles market.

Like all the Genesis and solo albums since 1972, I bought *Cured* the week it was released and to say I was disappointed would be a major understatement. Nonetheless, on the strength of the previous albums, it reached fifteen in the UK chart on 29 August 1981 and remained in the top 75 for five weeks. Steve later commented that it wasn't a deliberate attempt to write commercial songs; he was simply finding his way as a singer. The majority of fans, however, seemed to share my sentiments. It was one of the first albums to feature the Linndrum which had been launched the previous year.

August was a busy month for Steve; in addition to the album release, he returned to the annual Reading Festival as a 'special guest'. The performance was recorded, but – except for broadcast by the BBC – the full setlist went unreleased until 2016. A tour followed with future Marillion drummer Ian Mosley – who Steve had met at Redan Studios – and ex-Strawbs bassist Chas Cronk joining Magnus and the Hackett brothers. UK and European dates in August, September and October included the Soviet Bloc for the first time, followed by a trip to North America in November. Songs from *Cured*, specifically 'Hope I Don't Wake', 'Picture Postcard' and 'Funny Feeling' were not always well received, with the critic for the *Los Angeles Times* describing them as 'leaden'.

The fuzzy, holiday snap cover photo of Steve looks tacky but feels appropriate given the album's rudimentary feel.

'Hope I Don't Wake' 3:48 (Steve Hackett)

Cured is essentially a song-based album with a greater emphasis on lyrics than on previous releases. The songs are all sung in the first person by Steve and love – or the lack of it – is a core theme. The words to the opening track reveal that the song's insecure protagonist is in an uncertain relationship and fears that any day his partner will walk out on him. It was the first single from the album, released on 7 August 1981, but despite the bright, upbeat vibe and radio-friendly length, it failed to win over record buyers.

The song itself is at odds with the downbeat lyrics. The sunny chorus featuring Steve's multi-tracked, acapella harmonies owes an obvious debt to 'Carry On Wayward Son' by Kansas. There's even a hint of an American accent as Steve uses the style of Steve Walsh – with a touch of Crosby, Stills, Nash and Young – throughout the song. Musically, it features a lightweight arrangement of organ, jangly rhythm guitar and Linndrum. The melodic – but all too short – guitar break at 2:45 is a brief reminder of what Steve does best.

'Picture Postcard' 3:55 (Hackett)

Despite the title, this is not a reference to the idyllic locale of the cover artwork. Instead, the lyrics find our protagonist feeling lonely and craving for companionship. Again, the music tells a different story. Although Steve sings in a higher register – reminiscent of Roger Hodgson of Supertramp – the verses are a little more laid back than the previous song with an engaging, circular rhythm. At 1:23, it kicks up its heels for the song's uplifting chorus which surprisingly makes only one appearance. The mellow middle-eight at 2:34 with its fluid bass is also effective, bringing to mind some of the better UK pop acts of the early 80s. At 3:00, multi-instrumentalist Peter 'Bimbo' Acock plays out with a spirited, semi-improvised sax solo. Released in October 1981, 'Picture Postcard' was the second – and last – single from the album. Saleswise, it shared the same fate as its predecessor.

'Can't Let Go' 5:43 (Hackett)

The album's longest track opens with a subdued, tabla-like drum pattern before magisterial keyboard strings rise sun-like over the horizon. It's all very atmospheric, but the synth soon adopts a more mundane, early '80s tone and when the song kicks in proper at 1:45, we're back in AOR territory. Despite the uninspired chorus, the song has its moments including a superbly prominent bass line, sweet wordless harmonies, dexterous synth fills and a breezy – if very un-Hackett – guitar solo at 3:13. Steve's guitar is given an extended workout at 4:36, providing a lively, foot-tapping playout. The lyrics relate a sad case of obsessive – but unreciprocated – love.

'The Air-Conditioned Nightmare' 4:42 (Hackett)

The final track on side one of the original vinyl LP is the album's first instrumental; how times change! If I was beginning to feel that Steve had lost the plot with this album, back in 1981, this track did at least restore a semblance of faith.

It opens with howling, solo guitar with Steve overdosing on sustain. At 0:45, it breaks into a spiralling, organ and guitar-driven riff that echoes Emerson, Lake and Palmer in their prime although the lightweight drum sound lets the side down. The bass pedals also lack clout. At 2:15, a pounding bass line – think ELP's 'Fanfare for the Common Man' – ushers in a variation on the theme with guitar synth and keys blending to produce a relentless barrage. This track would not sound out of place as the theme for a movie thriller and there are shades of Henry Mancini's 'Peter Gunn' theme – without the twangy 1950s guitar. Unsurprisingly, this track transferred very successfully to the stage and certainly rocks harder, and more satisfyingly, when performed by a full band.

'Funny Feeling' 4:07 (Hackett, Nick Magnus)

Like 'The Air-Conditioned Nightmare', the opening song on side two made its live debut at the Reading Festival on 28th August 1981. Things are still not going well for our protagonist and here, his uncaring partner is about to walk out the door for good. Musically, it's hardly better news with a weak melody driven by a cod-disco rhythm, an uninspired synth tone and overripe vocals. Only the ringing guitar fills and a surprisingly heavyweight break at 2:19 engage, but even they fail to lift this above the ordinary. The melodic guitar solo at 3:29 that closes the song is welcome but sounds like it's been tacked on as an afterthought. This has early 1980s assembly-line pop-rock stamped all over it.

'A Cradle of Swans' 2:49 (Hackett)

This is the album's obligatory solo acoustic guitar instrumental, but it is a welcome diversion nonetheless. Beautifully and supremely played on nylon guitar, it harks back to previous solo offerings although it has a more classical, Spanish flavour. Although an original composition, it could almost be a traditional piece and the rapid fingering at 2:00 is breathtaking.

'Overnight Sleeper' 4:37 (Hackett, Kim Poor)

For a change, this is a song that eschews love and relationships as its subject. It's the first of several that Steve would record over the years that take trains – and steam trains in particular – as its theme. This is understandable given his passion for globetrotting and what better way of appreciating the splendours of a country than from the comfort of a train. On this occasion, however, it's a nightmare scenario where he's trying to outrun a speeding locomotive.

It continues from the previous track with a flurry of nylon guitar notes before Magnus' fiery synth line picks up the melody. The drum machine does a pretty good job of imitating the rhythm of a speeding train, sounding less synthetic than Steve's processed singing. The song's best element is a joyous Mexican dance theme that serves as the main hook. With cascading flute to the fore, it's very reminiscent of 'Jacuzzi' on *Defector* but like several songs here, the tone doesn't match the lyrics. Nonetheless, it's one of the album's best offerings, rounded off by a rampant and very proggy guitar and bass outro. Like 'The Air-Conditioned Nightmare', the song was successfully performed on the subsequent tour.

'Turn Back Time' 4:23 (Hackett)

Appropriately, another love song to close the album. Steve opts for a slow ballad to reflect the thoughts of his protagonist who's separated from his true love. Here, the three-part harmonies appear to be making a conscious attempt to mimic The Beach Boys and the rising wordless voices during the chorus are again evocative of 10cc's 1975 hit 'I'm Not In Love'. In fact, the song sounds like a 1970s pop throwback with mellow electric piano and guitar being the main instrumentation. The melody is good, but the arrangement really dates it, especially the limp drum sound. Overall, it's not the most inspired ending to a Steve Hackett album.

Related Tracks

The 2007 CD remaster of *Cured* on Virgin Records contains three bonus tracks.

'Tales of the Riverbank' 2:00 (Mauro Giuliani)

This delightful classical guitar tune takes me back to my childhood and BBC children's TV in the early 1960s. Steve believed the composer was unknown but later discovered it was by nineteenth-century guitar virtuoso Mauro

Giuliani. The actual title is 'Raccolta, op. 43, no. 6: Andante in C'. This version was first released as the B-side to the 'Hope I Don't Wake' single in August 1981 and Steve played it on the *Bay of Kings* acoustic tour in 1983.

'Second Chance' 2:00 (Hackett)

This is a haunting nylon guitar and flute duet featuring Steve and brother John. It was commissioned for the eponymous 1981 TV series *Second Chance* starring Susannah York and Ralph Bates and was originally released as the B-side to the 'Picture Postcard' single in October 1981 where it was listed as 'Theme from Second Chance'. It is also included on the 1983 *Bay of Kings* album and Steve has performed it numerous times live including the 'Acoustic trio' tours.

'The Air-Conditioned Nightmare' (Live) 4:08 (Hackett)

First released as the B-side to the 'Cell 151' single in March 1983, this was recorded at the Reading Festival on 28 August 1981 where it opened the set to a rapturous response. It was later a bonus track on the 2016 'Deluxe Edition' of *Defector*. It ranks alongside 'Clocks' and 'Slogans' as one of Steve's most powerful live workouts from this period and runs rings around the studio version.

Highly Strung (1983)

Personnel:
Steve Hackett: guitars, vocals
Nick Magnus: keyboards, devices
Ian Mosley: drums
Additional personnel:
Chris Lawrence: contrabass
Nigel Warren-Green: cello
Produced by: Steve Hackett, John Acock
Engineered by: John Acock, Rafe McKenna, Brad Grisdale
Recorded at: Berry Street Studios, Marcus Music, and Redan Recorders, London
Recording date: February – November 1982
Release date: 23 April 1983
Record label: UK: Charisma Records, USA: Epic Records
Highest chart places: UK: 16, USA: Did not chart
Running time: 37:01

1982 was a relatively lean year for Steve, but it had its moments. As mentioned, an offer to join Keith Emerson and Jack Bruce in a proposed 'supergroup' was turned down as was an offer to become an unlikely replacement for singer Paul Jones in a West End musical. Instead, he participated in several benefit events. On 2 October, he joined his former bandmates for the rain-soaked 'Six of the Best' concert at the Milton Keynes Bowl in aid of Peter Gabriel's deeply in debt WOMAD. A late addition to the line-up, Steve flew in from Brazil, but delays meant he only made it for the encores. On 13 December, he headlined the 'Medical Aid to Poland' charity concert in London with Judie Tuzke. On 29 January 1983, he and his band were joined on stage by Gabriel and Mike Rutherford at the Guildford Civic Hall to raise money for the Tadworth Children's Hospital.

Otherwise, 1982 was given over to preparing and recording material for his sixth studio album. It was Steve's last for Charisma, the label associated with both his and the Genesis albums of the 1970s. In response to demands from fans, Steve wanted to release a live album which Charisma rejected as they did the acoustic album he had begun recording in 1980. It was also the label's interference that resulted in the protracted, eighteen-month process of shaping the album. Steve had to fight for artistic control when the label suggested an independent producer to give the album a commercial edge. By this point, Charisma was no longer the innovative label that Tony Stratton-Smith had founded in 1969 and their disarray may have been partly due to the fact that they were in the process of being taken over by Virgin Records in 1983.

Despite the wrangles, it was another successful album, entering the UK chart at number sixteen on 30 April, although it remained in the top 60 for just three weeks. 'Cell 151' which preceded the album was a minor hit single reaching 66 in the UK chart on 2 April although its chart run was also short-lived. For the American release, the album had a different track sequence with longer, twelve-inch single versions of 'Cell 151' and 'Walking Through Walls' opening each side of the LP.

While not exactly a complete return to form and uneven at times, *Highly Strung* is a significant improvement on its predecessor. Like *Cured*, Steve handles all vocals along with bass and lead guitar, joined by touring band members Nick Magnus and Ian Mosley. Steve found recording as part of a core trio an easy process and praised the drummer for his contribution. Magnus for his part – along with co-producer John Acock – had become a vital part in the production of Steve's albums. The three studios in which they recorded had their own characteristics with Redan, in Steve's words, producing a 'fine woody guitar sound'. A UK tour in April and May was followed by European dates before Steve returned with yet another album and tour later that same year.

The surreal cover painting features Steve holding a guitar which appears to be melting as he plays. As a sign of the times, on an inner cover photo, Steve is a model of 1980s sartorial elegance, sporting a skinny tie, baggy trousers and jacket sleeves pushed up above his forearms.

'Camino Royale' 5:27 (Steve Hackett, Nick Magnus)

Steve describes the opening track as the album's cornerstone, comprising 'Latin grooves meet the blues'. It's set in New Orleans and the title is taken from a street that eighteenth-century Spanish colonists named 'Camino Real Y Muelle'. The song came to Steve one night when, unable to sleep following a show there, he found himself walking the city's eerily empty streets.

The intro finds Steve in heavy, prog-rock mode with all guns blazing and guitar and organ jostling for attention. It still sounds fresh by today's standards and would not be out of place on an album by contemporary prog artist Neal Morse. The Hammond organ played by Nick Magnus belonged to Eddie Hardin and was recorded at his Herne Place Studios in Sunningdale, Berkshire. Eddie had once been a member of the Spencer Davis Group and Steve enjoyed working with him. At 1:19, it eases into a shuffle groove for the song proper with a syncopated rhythm underpinning Steve's ghostly vocal. The chorus, doubled by keys, is not as memorable as it might be. Steve wrote the song part while Magnus was responsible for the recurring main theme. At 4:34, it concludes as it began with rampaging guitar and organ reaching a monumental crescendo.

'Camino Royale' became a popular stage song and was rearranged for the 2012 *Genesis Revisited II* album. Steve remains particularly fond of the song which lent its name to the record label he launched in the early nineties.

'Cell 151' 3:30 (Hackett)

Charisma were pressuring Steve for a hit single and this was his response. It was the first track on the album to be recorded – in February 1982 – and was released as a single on 25 March 1983, spending two weeks in the UK chart.

An extended version was released as a twelve-inch single – popular in the early 1980s – which replaced this seven-inch single edit on the 2007 CD reissue. To satisfy Charisma, no less than eight different mixes were presented for their approval. The song is dominated by Mosley's cymbal-less, gated drum sound. Phil Collins' 'In the Air Tonight' had been a worldwide hit in 1981 and its influence is plain to hear. However, it's the pulsating cello rhythm that drives the song about a man desperate to be free from his prison cell. The memorable vocal hook is embellished by superb guitar, synth and organ fills, so no wonder it was a hit of sorts.

The extended 6:25 version, heralded by siren-like guitar, follows the song part with a variety of solos. Steve's experimental, distorted guitar exercises are offset by Magnus' more melodic keyboard intrusions. The final twenty seconds are given over to the hypnotic, slowly fading rhythm.

'Always Somewhere Else' 4:01 (Hackett)

The first of three instrumentals on the album and unusually for Steve, this is essentially a jam. It opens with random electric guitar noodling over Magnus' improvised piano chords. The rhythm section enters at 1:33 for a jazz-flavoured workout reminiscent of the more melodic fusion bands of the 1970s like Brand X. It still boasts a core melody and it's a pretty good one at that, with Steve's buoyant guitar propelled by Mosley's relentless drumming – his best on the album. A Hammond organ has the final word, providing the unexpectedly-serene conclusion. One of the lesser-known highlights of Steve's career, it almost didn't make the album until Steve played it on a car stereo and realised how good it sounded. It has occasionally been resurrected for live performance – minus the slow intro.

'Walking Through Walls' 3:48 (Hackett)

Closing side one of the vinyl LP, we have an upbeat mainstream rock song that couples a driving rhythm with a sparse arrangement. Following a short drum solo intro, Mosley lays down a steady beat. Magnus' gritty electric piano riff is characteristic of Tony Banks' more simplified keyboard work with Genesis in the early '80s on songs like 'Turn It On Again' and 'That's All', while Steve's edgy vocal is almost unrecognisable and at 2:12, he offers his most bluesy and hard-hitting guitar solo thus far. The song's subject – overcoming life's obstacles through sheer grit and determination – came to Steve while taking his daily run by London's Holland Park. It's not one of his most inspired songs, it has to be said but certainly an improvement on some of the lightweight fodder that graced *Cured*. 'Walking Through Walls' was the proposed follow up single to 'Cell 151' as both a seven-inch and twelve-inch single, but the release failed to materialise.

'Give It Away' 4:07 (Hackett)

The side two opener hits the ground running with a majestic guitar theme setting the scene for the multi-tracked, AOR-style harmonies. Steve's vocals here are reminiscent of Trevor Rabin who made his Yes debut with 'Owner of a Lonely Heart' less than six months after the release of this album. Typically for Steve, the song's optimistic vibe is at odds with the lyrics, in which the broken-hearted protagonist has lost his first love. Compared with the previous track, this has a denser sound and the rhythm department – although well played – suffers as a result. There are no such problems for the guitars, with full-bodied acoustic chiming through at 2:20 and a razor-sharp electric solo cutting through the murk at 3:21, to provide a rousing coda.

'Weightless' 3:31 (Hackett)

Steve wrote this song about his experience of hang-gliding over Rio De Janeiro during a trip to Brazil. In keeping with the subject, it has a lighter than air feel, driven by a restrained drum pattern, piano and bass synth. Only the shouty, overeager vocals which are drenched in reverb and echo seem out of place. It's a decent enough tune, but is probably one of Steve's most disposable offerings, especially considering the absence of guitar. The album is loaded with songs that were clearly written and recorded as potential singles and at a radio-friendly three and a half minutes, this is one such track. Along with 'Camino Royale', 'Cell 151', 'Walking Through Walls' and 'Give It Away', 'Weightless' was played on the subsequent *Highly Strung* tour.

'Group Therapy' 5:47 (Hackett)

Although this also lives up to its name, it's another excursion into jazz-rock territory. The album's second instrumental – and longest track – it combines elements of fusion, an area rarely frequented by Steve, and prog – to convincing effect. It's fast, frantic and an impressively played throwback to 1970s pioneers like Frank Zappa, the Mahavishnu Orchestra and Chick Corea's Return to Forever. Underpinned by a restless rhythm and staccato chords with Mosley once again shining, the fiery guitar and synth exchanges develop into a duel at 1:32 with Steve and Magnus trying hard to outgun each other. At 3:30, it takes on a lighter, proggier dimension with a circular rhythm before guitar and keys make a final dash to the finish. By my estimation, it ends in a draw.

'India Rubber Man' 2:31 (Hackett)

Left breathless by the previous workout, Steve tones things down with this evocative ballad. Piano and keyboard strings combine to gorgeous effect, bringing to mind 'Hammer in the Sand' on *Defector.* Again, the vocals are heavy on the reverb, but this adds to the song's poignancy and the elusive lyrics which relate to someone in Steve's life who is 'bending the rules now and then'. The tasteful harmonica solo at 1:11 has a romantic touch of Americana about it, bringing to mind the more lyrical music of Copland, although, in fact, it recalls the main theme from 'Always Somewhere Else'. Had John Hackett been on the album, the solo would have probably been played on the flute but

45

I can't imagine it sounding better than this. Harmonica is an instrument Steve should feature more often in the future. Magnus concludes this all too brief song with a symphonic flourish. Without question, it's my favourite song on the album and one of Steve's best.

'Hackett to Pieces' 2:39 (Hackett, Magnus)

The album's closing track was also appropriately the last to be recorded – in October and November 1982. This is, in essence, an instrumental version of 'Camino Royale', reprising the main theme and key elements from the opening song. Here, the tone is less strident and more majestic with keyboards providing an added orchestral gloss. At 1:04, tribal drums and crashing chords enter the fray, building the tension to a guitar-charged peak before a descending synth line heralds the slow, drum-driven fade. It is a satisfying ending to a mostly satisfying album, bringing it full circle. This track, by the way, has nothing to do with 'Hackett to Bits' on the 1986 GTR album which is a variation of the 'Please Don't Touch' instrumental.

Related Tracks

The 2007 CD reissue of *Highly Strung* on Virgin Records contains the following three bonus tracks. The digital remastering was again by Benedict Fenner. The 2015 box-set *Premonitions: The Charisma Recordings 1975-1983* contains four previously unreleased live bonus tracks recorded on 4 March 1983 for BBC Radio One's *Friday Rock Show* hosted by Tommy Vance. The sixteen-minute session includes 'Cell 151', 'Walking Through Walls', 'Hackett to Pieces' and 'Please Don't Touch'.

'Guitar Boogie' 2:11 (Chuck Berry)

A rock and roll standard that was an occasional live encore at the time. Steve clearly had fun recording it with his frantic guitar salvos incorporating boogie, heavy metal and improv. John Hackett also plays guitar and Chas Cronk plays some nifty bass, as they did on stage.

'Walking Through Walls' (12" version) 5:55 (Hackett)

This is an extended version remixed by Rafe McKenna at George Martin's Air Studios for a proposed twelve-inch single. It boasts a more punchy sound with the usual delay and repeat effects characteristic of twelve-inch mixes of the early '80s. The most notable addition is the stirring synth and drums march at 4:46 that concludes the track.

'Time Lapse at Milton Keynes' 3:52 (Hackett)

This piece was originally released on the B-side of the 'Cell 151' twelve-inch single in March 1983. Steve wrote and recorded it to commemorate the WOMAD reunion with his ex-Genesis bandmates in October 1982. It is another of his delicate classical guitar pieces with a haunting melody. It's a shame it wasn't on the original album although it was perhaps considered to be one instrumental too many.

Bay of Kings (1983)

Personnel:
Steve Hackett: acoustic guitars, keyboard strings
John Hackett: flutes
Nick Magnus: synthesiser, keyboard strings, effects
Produced by: Steve Hackett, John Acock
Recorded and mixed by John Acock
Recorded at: Berry Street Studios and The Town House, London
Recording date: 1980 – 1983
Release date: October 1983
Record label: UK: Lamborghini Records, USA: Chrysalis Records
Highest chart places: UK: 70, USA: Did not chart
Running time: 44:26

Bay of Kings was Steve's first mostly acoustic album and his second album of 1983, following *Highly Strung* by just six months. Charisma had rejected the album, so Steve severed his ties with the label he had been with since 1971 when he joined Genesis. In the UK, it was released on the recently-launched Lamborghini Records, a division of PRT Records, the label owner Patric Mimran being better known for his prestigious car company. Although his first all-acoustic recordings as an album, Steve had been inspired to play classical guitar at the age of fifteen after hearing recordings by the virtuoso Segovia and as a result he devoted hours to practice.

Steve began recording the album in 1980 before being diverted by the *Cured* album and *Bay Of Kings* combines new instrumentals with re-arranged versions of popular solo guitar pieces including 'Horizons' and 'Kim'. Styles on the album include classical, folk and flamenco with nylon guitar strongly featured, although he used steel strings where he felt the pieces required a brighter tone. Steve described the acoustic guitar as 'a small orchestra', allowing him to produce a variety of textures, moods and dynamics. He credits his broad technique to being self-taught and uses the nylon guitar, in particular, to impersonate the sound of other instruments, especially the piano. Several of the tracks are inspired by the sea while others paint images of landscapes and a bygone age. Following his absence from the previous album, John Hackett returns, joining Steve for the guitar and flute duets. Nick Magnus provides the string samples, adding a romantic, classical feel at times.

Despite spending just one week in the UK chart on 19 November 1983, the album was well-received by fans and critics alike. The tranquil mood was a welcome respite from the synth-pop and stadium rock prevalent at the time. It also predates the popular 'unplugged' recordings by numerous artists that followed. The release was accompanied by a solo tour of the UK through October and November, playing mostly universities. A performance at Edinburgh's Queens Hall on 4 November was released in 2006 as *Live Archive 83*.

It's ironic that Steve chose to release an acoustic album in 1983 when his talents as a lead guitarist were influencing a host of new bands under the 'New Wave of Progressive Rock' banner. Leading exponents of 'neo-prog' – as it was later dubbed – like Marillion, Twelfth Night and IQ – acknowledged their debt to Genesis and Steve's playing in particular.

The painting of the reclining female nude on the original LP cover was one of Kim Poor's most artistic creations. Perhaps considered too risqué for the later CD reissues, it was later replaced by a portrait of Steve playing a classical guitar entitled 'The Small Orchestra'.

'Bay of Kings' 4:52 (Steve Hackett)
For the opening title track, Steve had in mind a slow-motion dance or a boat gently rising and falling on the ocean waves. It certainly reflects the track's elegant majesty with solo nylon guitar ebbing and flowing to a graceful, circular melody. The rippling arpeggios at 4:26 are a delight and perfectly in keeping with the mood of the piece.

'The Journey' 4:11 (Hackett)
A wave of orchestral keys introduces this haunting piece where – despite the title – nylon guitar is both hesitant and reflective. Here, the full-bodied, flamenco arpeggios at 2:02 lend the piece a Spanish feel, reflecting Steve's love of the country and its people. The combination of guitar and keyboard strings at 3:18 brings to mind the slow, second movement from Rodrigo's guitar 'Concierto de Aranjuez'. Simply stunning.

'Kim' 2:23 (Hackett)
A re-arranged version of one of Steve's best known acoustic pieces that originally featured on the 1978 *Please Don't Touch!* album. John makes his first appearance on the album, originating the harmony flute line. With John playing the melody, Steve mostly plays chords, underpinned by Magnus' swaying strings. The end result is the best version of this much-loved piece.

'Marigold' 3:33 (Hackett)
Steve reverts to a steel-strung guitar for this track in keeping with the bright, colourful image of the flower in question. Played on a six-string instrument, he utilised a harmoniser which makes it sound like a twelve-string, especially the chiming effect at 1:53. Tone-wise, it goes through several transitions, even briefly sounding like a guitar synth at 2:22.

'St. Elmo's Fire' 3:06 (Hackett)
This piece is not to be confused with the AOR power ballad of the same name which appeared less than two years later. In contrast with 'Bay of Kings', it reflects the sea at its most turbulent. Another solo guitar piece, Steve detuned

both E strings to D to create the unusual chord inversions. Although melody light, it has a dramatic, rhythmic quality that makes for compelling listening.

'Petropolis' 2:44 (Hackett)

Opening side two of the original vinyl LP, this piece was written during a rainstorm in Petropolis, a Brazilian city north of Rio de Janeiro. The spikey notes in this solo guitar exercise do a pretty good rain imitation. Despite the South American setting, at around the one minute mark the piece breaks into a courtly, Renaissance-style melody. Naggingly familiar, it's reminiscent of Nina Rota's incidental music for the 1968 film version of *Romeo and Juliet*.

'Second Chance' 1:56 (Hackett)

A piece previously discussed, this was written as a theme for the 1981 TV series of the same name starring Ralph Bates and Susannah York. An evocative nylon guitar and flute duet, it was originally released as the B side to the October 1981 single 'Picture Postcard'.

'Cast Adrift' 2:11 (Hackett)

Here, Steve evokes the timeless beauty of the sea and its shores. Another solo guitar piece, it's both delicate one moment and all chiming chord-clusters the next. The melody is one of the most memorable on the album that again has that 'I'm sure I've heard this somewhere before' quality.

'Horizons' 1:44 (Hackett)

Steve's first piece written for solo acoustic guitar, inspired by John Renborn and his song 'Sir John a Lot of'. It was the opening track on side two of Genesis' 1972 *Foxtrot* album and was thereafter always associated with the epic 'Supper's Ready' that immediately followed with barely a pause. Here, it's played a little slower and softer than the original but loses none of its potency.

'Black Light' 2:29 (Hackett)

Steve described the arpeggios and chords on this solo guitar track as 'note clusters'. Again, he creates a shimmering, rhythmic effect that trades melody for dramatic effect but is totally compelling all the same. He has regularly performed this piece live over the years, often as part of an acoustic medley.

'The Barren Land' 3:43 (Hackett)

This piece was inspired by Steve's journey through Spain's Basque territory en route to San Sebastian. Despite the title, the solo nylon guitar timbre is rich and fulsome with a sprightly theme that, unsurprisingly, has a Spanish flavour. The sudden shifts between the slow and fast passages around the midsection are nothing short of breathtaking.

'Calmaria' 3:22 (Hackett)

To close the album, this is a gentle, reflective piece, again influenced by Steve's travels. The title is a Portuguese word meaning calm or in Steve's translation, the calm after the storm. And that's exactly what the music conveys with pastoral nylon guitar notes cascading over stately keyboard strings. The understated orchestral finale is magical.

Related Tracks

Bay of Kings was reissued on CD in 1998 on Steve's own Camino Records label. It includes three bonus tracks recorded and mixed by Richard Buckland. A 30th Anniversary reissue in 2013 features the same tracks.

'Time Lapse at Milton Keynes' 3:56 (Hackett)

This is a solo guitar piece inspired by the Genesis stage reunion in October 1982 to fund Peter Gabriel's ailing WOMAD. It was also a bonus track on the 2007 CD reissue of *Highly Strung* – see the previous chapter.

'Tales of the Riverbank' 2:02 (Mauro Giuliani)

Like the author, as a young boy in the early 60s, Steve was a fan of BBC TV's *Tales of the Riverbank* and this sweet classical guitar tune that accompanied it. It was released as the B-side to the 'Hope I Don't Wake' single in August 1981 and Steve played it on the *Bay of Kings* acoustic tour.

'Skye Boat Song' 1:35 (Traditional)

Another nineteenth-century tune, although this is better known as a stirring, Scottish ballad celebrating Charles Edward Stuart – better known as Bonnie Prince Charlie. Steve first played this on the harmonica as a young boy and it was his mother's favourite. His tasteful solo guitar rendition of this bittersweet tune is an absolute delight.

Till We Have Faces (1984)

Personnel:
Steve Hackett: guitars, Roland GR-300 guitar synth, koto, rainstick, Etruscan guitar, marimba, percussion, harmonica, vocals
Nick Magnus: keyboards, percussion, drum programming
Additional personnel:
Rui Mota: drums
Sérgio Lima: drums
Ian Mosley: drums, percussion
Waldemar Falcão: flute, percussion
Fernando Moura: Rhodes piano
Ronaldo Diamante: bass
Clive Stevens: wind synthesiser
Kim Poor: Japanese voice on 'A Doll That's Made in Japan'
The Brazilian Percussionists: Sidinho Moreira, Junior Homrich, Jaburu, Peninha, Zizinho, Baca
Produced by Steve Hackett, John Acock, Nick Magnus, Waldemar Falcão
Engineered by: Rio: Carlos E. Cesar, Andy P. Mills, Felipe Nery, Waldemar Falcão.
London: John Acock, Gwyn Mathias
Recorded at: Som Livre Studios, Rio de Janeiro and Marcus Music Studios, London except 'Doll' at Silo
Recording date: 1983 – 1984
Release date: 7 September 1984
Record label: UK: Lamborghini Records, USA: Chrysalis Records
Highest chart places: UK: 54, USA: Did not chart
Running time: 41:02

Steve had been spending a good deal of time in Brazil in recent years, absorbing the country's culture. Indeed, as a musician, it seemed a natural progression to incorporate South American rhythms into his own compositions. The result, *Till We Have Faces* was Steve's most left-field offering yet. The album takes its title from C.S. Lewis' last novel, published in 1956. The work of the same author also influenced the song 'Narnia' that opened the *Please Don't Touch!* album.

Several of the local musicians were street performers but getting them organised in the studio wasn't easy. Recorded mostly in Rio, he could only get studio time after midnight and was never entirely sure who would turn up. But the musicians enjoyed the sessions so much that Steve had to insist they take payment, with Nick Magnus the only British musician working with him in Brazil. The recording was completed in London and mixed by co-producer John Acock using Ambisonics, an early surround-sound system, which produced a wider sound field than stereo to give the illusion of the listener being in the studio. Brazillian musician and engineer Waldemar Falcão came to London to assist in unravelling and mixing the complex rhythm tracks with

Steve acknowledging that the whole experience was something he would never be able to repeat.

Unfairly, the album was dismissed by many critics and fans as an unsuccessful marriage of world music and the overtly commercial tendencies on *Cured*. It spent just two weeks in the UK top 100 in September 1984. It was Steve's first album to be released on both vinyl and CD and was preceded by the single 'A Doll That's Made in Japan'. He was scheduled to appear at the Lilford Festival in Northamptonshire on 25 August – his first gig with a full band that year – but the festival was cancelled at the eleventh hour when the local council refused to issue a license. Given the spontaneity of the performances, *Till We Have Faces* remains one of only a few Hackett albums that was never performed live. Although he later felt that it might have contained even more world music, Steve remained proud of the album, as was clear from his notes in the booklet for the 1994 CD reissue, which features a different track sequencing to the one below.

The cover painting is a sombre effort, depicting ghostly figures in a small boat shrouded in mist. It was inspired by the haunting instrumental 'Silent Sorrow in Empty Boats' on the Genesis *The Lamb Lies Down on Broadway* album.

'Duel' 4:48 (Steve Hackett)

The opening song is based on Steven Spielberg's tense 1971 thriller *Duel*. It was the director's feature-length debut as a director and the plot concerns an innocent motorist terrorised by a faceless truck driver. While the film ends on a triumphant note, the song leaves the story hanging in the air with the chilling final line 'Will this killer win and run you off the road?'.

Musically we're on familiar, mainstream rock ground with a shuffle rhythm and a pulsating electric piano riff. Guitar darts in and out with police car siren-like calls and there's an ominous foreboding in Steve's otherwise-smooth vocal. He utilises various guitar devices to create the sound effects including a Gizmo at the beginning to simulate a starting motor and an E-bow for the wailing fills. The roar of the truck's engine is courtesy of Magnus' keyboard effects. The lengthy solo at 2:42 which closes the song makes effective use of Steve's familiar hammering technique.

'Matilda Smith-Williams Home for the Aged' 8:04 (Hackett, Nick Magnus)

A contender for Steve's longest song title is also one of his longest tracks. It was inspired by an old folks home in the Caribbean, although the location could actually be anywhere, containing as it does irreverent lines like 'And if you smuggle in another drop of gin, we'll take your hearing aid away'. The subject and words, however, are little more than an excuse for some superb musicianship, especially the all-instrumental final five minutes.

The howling guitar tone from the previous track is reprised for the intro before the song motors along in a proggy vein with a brisk organ-led rhythm and synth embellishments. Steve's multi-tracked vocals place it firmly in the

53

mid-1980s, but the stirring guitar work is timeless. The song comes to a dead stop of 3:05, allowing the unaccompanied Brazilian drummers to demonstrate their percussive talents. As it develops into a samba rhythm, they are joined by a majestic synth theme at 5:04 which builds to a stirring crescendo. Lead guitar and guitar synth enter at 6:24, doubling the synth line, playing to exhilarating effect before the final fade. This is one of Steve's most satisfying tracks since the *Defector* album that fully justifies its eight-minute playing time. It was substantially remixed for the 1994 CD reissue.

'Let Me Count the Ways' 6:05 (Hackett)

As Monty Python's John Cleese used to say, and now for something completely different. Following a barely discernible count-in by drummer Rui Mota in Portuguese, this is a slow, twelve-bar blues song where Steve's mannered singing sounds uncannily like Robert Plant in places. The guitar playing harks back to his roots and blues greats like B.B. King and John Lee Hooker. The lyrics affectionately parody a stereotypical blues ballad with lines like 'I'm a mess without your love, baby blue'. Even at six minutes plus, the song has a certain charm and glides by before you know it. Inside the booklet with the 1994 CD reissue, under the song title, it says 'For Uncle Charlie', a tribute perhaps to a recently departed relative?

'A Doll That's Made in Japan' 3:56 (Hackett)

Like 'The Red Flower of Tachai Blooms Everywhere' on *Spectral Mornings,* this song is resplendent with oriental flourishes, although it's a far more rhythmic affair. According to Steve's sleeve notes, the rhythm which originates from Brazil is called a Baião. I'll take his word for it. Either way, it's a lively, syncopated song in which the Brazilian percussionists combine with conventional rock drums, keyboards and a pumping bass line. Steve plays the koto for the lilting solo intro and it's a reasonably successful marriage of oriental and South American timbres, although the organ stabs that punctuate the verses are straight out of the shower scene from *Psycho.* In keeping with the theme, the lyrics are awash with Japanese references including samurai, sushi and the streets of Tokyo. Despite the influences, it was recorded in London during the album's final sessions.

It was released as a single in August 1984 prior to the album but to no success. The seven-inch version featured an instrumental version of the A-side as the B-side. The twelve-inch version released in the UK and parts of Europe boasted an extended 5:55 version as the A-side and a different track 'Just the Bones' on the B-side.

'Myopia' 2:54 (Hackett, Magnus)

For record buyers still committed to vinyl, this was the opening track on side two of the original LP. It's a storming, cod-punk / heavy metal workout where Steve's tongue is firmly planted in his cheek. His vocal is suitably breathless, especially during the repetitive choral hook. The title and lyrics refer to his own short-sightedness; from his school days to his early years with Genesis he wore spectacles and more recently, contact lenses. To prove they're not taking themselves too seriously, at 1:51 there's a convincingly performed extract from the 'Allegro' of Bach's 'Brandenburg Concerto No. 3' courtesy of Magnus' keyboard strings. When performed live as an instrumental, 'Myopia' was occasionally a rousing set opener. It was resurrected for the 2017-2019 *Genesis Revisited* tours where it was part of a medley with 'Slogans' and 'Los Endos'.

'What's My Name' 7:04 (Hackett, Magnus)

This is side two's long song, and it's another world music offering that wears its oriental and South American influences on its sleeve. Steve was inspired to write it after reading the book *Six Records of a Floating Life* by Fu Shen. Musically, he describes the song as 'Ancient China meets Amazonian Brazil.'

Compared with 'A Doll That's Made in Japan', this is a more hypnotic, slow-burning track despite the imposing percussive sounds, with Brazilian percussionist Junior Homrich responsible for the mesmerising, clock-like rhythm that opens the song. He had greater fame as a composer and was later nominated for an Oscar for the soundtrack to the 1985 film *The Emerald Forest*. At 2:24, march-like percussion ushers in Steve's multi-tracked vocals where the wordless choral harmonies sound remarkably like Jon Anderson. In fact, this track would not sound out of place on one of the former Yes singer's solo albums. Magnus provides the suitably exotic synth embellishments and his vibrant, keyboard orchestrations that conclude the track are simply stunning.

'The Rio Connection' 3:19 (Hackett)

This is an aptly titled instrumental that was mostly recorded live in the studio. It opens with the sound of the British telephone speaking clock, which remains an institution to this day despite the advent of digital timepieces and mobile phones. A nimble bass loop ushers in a jazzy groove with guitar, harmonica and synth soloing spontaneously over the solid, unified rhythm of drummers Rui Mota and Sérgio Lima. It's an agreeable diversion, but it's probably the album's most dispensable track.

'Taking the Easy Way Out' 3:48 (Hackett)

The title is a reference to alcohol as a sure-fire method for inducing sleep, which in this case brings on dreams of Egypt and distant lands. Appropriately, the song has a tranquil, dream-like quality with Steve's lush, multi-tracked harmonies on a cushion of mellow synths, harp-like nylon guitar and soft cymbal rolls. It is a track that's easy to overlook, but I'm a sucker for a haunting melody and this classically-structured song – or should I say lullaby – certainly has that. It would have made a suitable album closer, but the album has one final track up its sleeve.

'When You Wish Upon a Star' 0:48 (Ned Washington, Leigh Harline)

In the same way that John Williams used it in the end title music for *Close Encounters of the Third Kind*, this is a homage to the famous 1940 theme from *Pinocchio* which became Walt Disney's signature tune. Magnus' analogue synths adopt a vintage sound that's both sweet and convincing without any hint of mocking.

Related Tracks

Till We Have Faces was reissued on CD in 1994 and later with a different track sequencing and two additional songs, 'The Gulf' and 'Stadiums of the Damned'. Both songs were included on the *Feedback 86* album released in 2000 and are discussed in that chapter.

'Just the Bones' 5:58 (Hackett)

This was the B-side on the twelve-inch single of 'A Doll That's Made in Japan' released in the UK and parts of Europe. It did not appear on *Till We Have Faces* and has never been released on CD. The bare-bones – if you excuse the pun – lyrics are centred around the title against a thudding drum track. It has a hypnotic, new-age groove with worldless choral voices supported by piano and symphonic keys. The sparse melody is understated but memorable nonetheless. Only the scratchy, discordant guitar volleys that enter at 3:38 outstay their welcome, spoiling the ambient mood. Otherwise, it's a perfect accompaniment for the A-side.

Momentum (1988)

Personnel:
Steve Hackett: guitar, keyboards
John Hackett: flute
Produced by Steve Hackett, John Acock
Engineered by John Acock
Recorded at: Raezor Studios, London
Recording date: 1987 – 1988
Release date: 28 March 1988
Record label: Start Records
Highest chart places: UK: Did not chart, USA: Did not chart
Running time: 41:02

The three and a half year gap between *Momentum* and its predecessor was the longest between successive Hackett solo albums to that point. He was far from idle in the interim period, however. In 1985, at the suggestion of ex-Yes manager Brian Lane, Steve formed the aptly named GTR with former Yes guitarist Steve Howe and the pair wrote songs together for a proposed album. In February 1986, he made his first live appearance in over two years, joining Marillion for a charity gig at London's Hammersmith Odeon performing the perennial 'I Know What I Like'. The GTR single 'When the Heart Rules the Mind' released in March and the subsequent self-titled album were both hits, especially in America. A sell-out tour of North America and Europe concluded at the Hammersmith Odeon on 14 September 1986.

Saleswise, 1986 was a peak year for Genesis and its ex-members. *Invincible Touch* was a number one album in the UK and the band had four top-five hits in the USA. Peter Gabriel's *So* also reached the top of the UK album chart and 'Sledgehammer' was a *Billboard* number-one single. Despite GTR's flush of success, Steve was unwilling to commit to a full-time group environment. So, in 1986 and 1987, he wrote and recorded what would have been his follow-up to *Till We Have Faces*. The sessions featured several guest musicians and singers, harking back to *Please Don't Touch!*, but due to contractual issues, however, the album would not see the light of day until October 2000.

Following the GTR experience, business resumed as normal for Steve with a far more personal album, *Momentum*. He made the decision that every few years he would record a classically-styled, acoustic album in the vein of *Bay of Kings* and without huge commercial success in mind. Compared with that album, however, the playing is more intricate; he was deliberately pushing himself as a guitarist. It showcases Steve's talents as a nylon guitar maestro as well as John's beautiful flute playing, even though the majority of the tracks are solo offerings. This time out, he was particularly influenced by Andalusian and Moorish music and aptly labelled it 'music without props'. With Lamborghini Records folding in 1985, *Momentum* saw another change of label for Steve and it was also the last album co-produced by John Acock who had worked with Steve since his 1975 debut.

Momentum was well received by supporters and pundits alike with respectable sales, despite a lack of chart success; it was Steve's first album not to breach the UK Top 100. A twenty date tour of the UK followed in April and May 1988 with Steve and John performing in relatively intimate venues like the Manchester Opera House and London's Sadler's Wells Theatre. The tour continued across Europe in May and following a summer break, resumed in the autumn, culminating with a trip to the Soviet Union to a reputed crowd of over 90,000.

The simple but effective cover artwork captures a couple in an intimate moment, reflecting the romanticism of the music.

'Cavalcanti' 6:13 (Steve Hackett)

For the delicate opening section of this piece, Steve was inspired by the ornate Moorish palaces of Spain. The rippling fingering technique at 2:50 that evokes running water is supremely executed, while to perfect the rapid, up and down arpeggios at 3:40 portraying galloping horses, he had to practise exceptionally hard. John enters at 4:45 for a delightful closing flute melody, buoyed by keyboard strings.

'The Sleeping Sea' 3:26 (Hackett)

This is one of Steve's favourite tracks on the album. It incorporates a descending note sequence and what he describes as 'Moorish harmonies' and his playing here is measured and a little dryer than usual. The slightly dissonant tone was to evoke the sea at night and the predators that lurk in the ocean's depths. The bell-like chord at the end was inspired by Claude Debussy's 1910 prelude 'La Cathédrale Engloutie' ('The Submerged Cathedral').

'Portrait of a Brazilian Lady' 5:14 (Hackett)

This is an evocative piece, full of light and shade and an irrepressible melody. Despite the leisurely pace, this piece has a spring in its steep, incorporating several twists and turns along the way. This is not as you might think, dedicated to Kim, but to her grandmother.

'When the Bell Breaks' 3:03 (Hackett)

This is one of my favourite pieces with a repeated, circular melody that's quite hypnotic. Here Steve adopts a tremolo, flamenco technique playing the top line with three fingers and the bass notes with the thumb. It gives the impression of two guitars playing rather than one, with the bottom strings sounding not unlike a mandolin.

'A Bed, a Chair and a Guitar' 2:42 (Traditional)

Harking back to Steve's teenage years where he spent many hours in his room practising, the title quotes his father who said that his son would be quite happy in life if all he had was a bed, a chair and a guitar. It is based on a traditional piece titled 'Nicola' as played by Bert Jansch that incorporates various playing styles. It begins in a classically baroque style followed by a lively folk-dance sequence at 0:31 before hitting its stride in jazzier style at 1:12.

'Concert for Munich' 4:54 (Hackett)

This was originally commissioned for a proposed film about the 1958 Munich air disaster that decimated the Manchester United football team. It has an expansive, cinematic arrangement with a stately synth strings theme preluding a haunting guitar and flute melody at 1:24. Steve dedicated the piece to Charisma Records boss Tony Stratton-Smith who had been a sports journalist in the 1950s and who passed away on 19 March 1987, one year before the release of *Momentum.*

'Last Rites of Innocence' 5:26 (Hackett)

A piece influenced by the classical Baroque style of Bach. Steve's nylon guitar – his 'small orchestra' – attempts to recreate the timbre of a string quartet by highlighting the different bass lines while playing the top strings. The end result is mostly successful, sounding delightfully light and airy. With such a striking melody, it would not sound out of place as the theme to a Jane Austen-type costume drama, set in the eighteenth century.

'Troubled Spirit' 2:30 (Hackett)

Despite the title, this is an optimistic, almost spiritual piece that suggests that troubles can be overcome by a stout heart. Steve's playing here is both elegant and intricate, with fast fingering exercises interspersed with pauses to indicate moments of quiet reflection. It is a sheer delight, that finishes all too soon.

'Variation on a Theme by Chopin' 4:55 (Hackett)

Although credited to Steve, this has a naggingly familiar theme, inspired by the romantic nineteenth-century style of Frédéric Chopin. Here, Steve attempts to evoke the tone of a piano and Chopin's gentle touch, in particular. The end result sounds like a classical guitar in places, a harp in others and around the midway point, a piano. It's beautifully written, arranged and played, showcasing the acoustic Hackett at his absolute best.

'Pierrot' 2:52 (Hackett)

The first track recorded for the album, this gentle, meditative piece portrays the famous single-teared clown as a doll that comes to life in the hands of a playful child. Similar to, 'When the Bell Breaks', Steve adopts a combined tremolo and bass note technique to replicate two separate guitars playing in unison.

'Momentum' 2:41 (Hackett)
Appropriately, the closing title track was the last piece written for the album. It's a lively solo guitar outing that suggests happy, carefree days beneath the Spanish sun. At the halfway mark, it comes close to reprising the acoustic guitar theme from the latter part of 'Racing in A'. It is a suitably bright, upbeat note on which to end the album.

Related Tracks
Momentum was reissued on CD in 1994 by Steve's then label, Camino Records. It included three bonus tracks, as did later reissues.

'Bourée' 1:34 (Johann Sebastian Bach)
A delightful solo guitar meditation that showcases Bach's use of bass notes and a proliferation of chords.

'An Open Window' 9:02 (Hackett)
This almost made it onto the original album but no doubt its nine-minute length counted against it. Steve didn't set out to write a long piece; it just evolved that way. He runs the full gamut of his acoustic guitar talents with gentle meditations rubbing shoulders with brittle, rhythmic interludes – accompanied by a drum track – and Spanish guitar flurries. As such, the title is wholly appropriate, while the opening and closing melody is also excellent.

'The Vigil' 6:19 (Hackett)
According to Steve, this was written and played in the 'Venetian' style to suggest the warmth and glow of candlelight. Even more so than 'Variation on a Theme by Chopin', the top bass strings produce a very convincing piano sound. In the first part, the single note melody has a haunting quality and in the second half, he again replicates a guitar-duet effect. This is Steve's acoustic playing at its most understated, yet it is still totally absorbing.

Guitar Noir (1993)

Personnel:
Steve Hackett: guitar, vocals, Stepp guitar synth, noises off, harmonica, string arrangements, rainstick
Julian Colbeck: keyboards on various, backing vocals on 'Little America'
Dave 'Taif' Ball: bass
Hugo Degenhardt: drums
Aron Friedman: keyboards, programming, string arrangements
Nick Magnus: keyboards, programming on 'Theatre of Sleep'
Bimbo Acock: clarinet on 'Theatre of Sleep'
Billy Budis: backing vocals on 'Paint Your Picture'
Produced by Steve Hackett, Aron Friedman, Billy Budis
Engineered by Aron Friedman, Billy Budis, Gerry O'Riordan, Jerry Peal
Recorded at: The Basement
Recording date: 1991 – 1993
Release date: May 1993
Record label: UK: Kudos by Permanent Records, USA: Viceroy Music
Highest chart places: UK: Did not chart, USA: Did not chart
Running time: 57:34

Following the *Momentum* tour, Steve almost dropped off the radar as far as fans were concerned. He spent part of 1989 and '90 establishing his own recording studio in Twickenham, a project he'd been planning for some time. He continued to participate in charity events including masterminding an all-star version of 'Sailing' for 'Rock Against Repatriation'. Recorded in December 1989 and released in February 1990, it was created in aid of the Vietnamese boat people who were making headline news at the time. Despite exhaustive promotion by Steve, sales of the single were not as good as he had hoped.

1992 saw the release of two albums, *The Unauthorised Biography* compilation followed by the long-awaited – and aptly titled – live album *Time Lapse*. The latter was the first taste of Steve's long and fruitful association with keyboardist Julian Colbeck who had also toured with Anderson Bruford Wakeman Howe. It also prompted a long-overdue tour of America, featuring songs from the next studio album in the set. The highlight of 1992, however, as far as Steve was concerned, was a prestigious performance of a Vivaldi Guitar Concerto with the London Chamber Orchestra at London's South Bank.

Guitar Noir was Steve's tenth studio recording and his first rock album in almost nine years. In the interim, CD had replaced vinyl as the primary listening format and as a result, it's significantly longer than any of his previous albums. While it failed to trouble the charts, it was warmly received and holds up as his best rock album since *Defector* in 1980. In addition to Colbeck, Steve's touring band from 1992 made their recording debut. Hugo Degenhardt was a session drummer of repute while bassist Dave Ball's diverse CV included Jon Hiseman and Killing Joke. Several songs were co-written with keyboardist and co-producer Aron Friedman while others were developed in the studio with the new band. Steve also recorded tracks with his manager and co-producer Billy Budis. On previous albums, the songs and instrumentals generally favoured either acoustic or electric guitars, but here Steve made a conscious effort to integrate both elements of his playing. Producer, engineer John Acock is conspicuous by his absence and the input of formerly ubiquitous keyboardist Nick Magnus is noticeably more low key.

The 1993 tour, launched in May, was Steve's most extensive in six years, taking in the UK, North and South America and Europe. The new band went down well with audiences and the new album was heavily featured in the first half of the set before making way for more familiar numbers later. Steve's main guitar was still his Gibson Les Paul custom with a Floyd Rose tremolo arm for a brighter tone. A performance recorded at London's The Grand Theatre on 8 June was released in 2001 as part of *Live Archive 70s 80s 90s.*

The original 1993 UK and European release of *Guitar Noir* featured a different track sequencing to the American version which also had the hidden track 'Cassandra'. To add to the confusion, it was later resequenced and the song 'Theatre of Sleep' added. It's this version I've used for the purposes of this sequence. Steve was rarely in the habit of putting demos on his albums, but he makes an exception here.

The cover artwork features Kim Poor's familiar enamel style painting on steel with Steve peering at the listener through a triangular-shaped aperture.

'Sierra Quemada' 5:19 (Steve Hackett)

To open the album is another of Steve's expansive instrumentals, allowing the listener's imagination to run free and conjure up their own images. The title is loosely translated as 'the scorched earth'. Steve himself likened the music to a condor with its wide wingspan soaring gracefully over the Peruvian mountains. Hugo Degenhardt's cymbal ride introduces the soaring guitar melody, which is up and running from the word go, demonstrating that Steve had clearly not been idle as far as practising went, as this is some of his most assured playing ever. He uses an ebow to great effect to produce the extended notes and Julian Colbeck's similarly sustained keyboard strings at 3:53 are heavenly.

This is a stunning instrumental that quite rightly became a stage favourite. It opens the second disc of the 2CD *Somewhere in South America...Live In Buenos Aires* album released in 2002. A 4:31 'demo' version of 'Sierra Quemada' is a bonus track on the 1997 reissue of *Guitar Noir* and features Steve's manager Billy Budis on bass.

'Take These Pearls' 4:14 (Hackett, Aron Friedman)

Steve is again responsible for the lead vocals on the album and his singing has rarely sounded better than it does here. It's a very atmospheric, spacey song, sounding quite unlike anything he had recorded previously. The subject is also atypical. A man is prepared to offer up priceless jewels to the one he loves. The lengthy intro features a myriad of percussive effects courtesy of Aron Friedman's keyboards. He is also responsible for the expansive orchestral arrangement and the ambient synth solo at 0:49, which brings to mind Vangelis tonally and, in particular, his soundtrack music for *Blade Runner*. Piano underpins Steve's multi-tracked, reverb-laden vocals and he also adds some sparse, but dexterous, classical guitar picking.

Sounding very much like studio creations, both 'Take These Pearls' and the following song 'There are Many Sides to the Night' transferred surprisingly successfully to the stage and were performed on the 1993 tour. A 4:11 'rough mix' of this song is a bonus track on the 1997 CD reissue.

'There are Many Sides to the Night' 7:23 (Hackett)
The tranquil mood continues with this track. In Steve's view, this and 'Dark as the Grave' are the album's most personal and atmospheric songs. It's a portrait of a prostitute and the moral of the story is that we should never judge a person by outward appearances – or their chosen profession. This time, it's the Stepp guitar synth that provides the lush string sounds and a hint of flute – used by Steve for the first time on this album. It provides a perfect counterpoint to the banshee-like guitar solo, replaced by nylon guitar at 1:52 before the vocals make their entrance at 2:35. These are spoken, rather than sung by Steve, interspersed by beautiful classical soloing. When he does begin singing at 4:01, his voice remains slow and meditative, perfectly in tune with the song's dreamy ambience. The wordless harmonies that follow the verses are a delight, as is the whole song. This is another richly atmospheric creation from Steve that demonstrates his developing maturity as a songwriter and arranger. It also provided the title to his 1995 acoustic live album, even though this song doesn't appear on it.

'In The Heart of the City' 4:35 (Hackett)
There's a change of pace for this song, which perfectly captures the hustle and bustle of busy city streets complete with the sound of a police siren at 1:54 and a radio traffic bulletin at 2:35. It brings to mind New York in the rush hour. It's the album's first conventional rock song although there is nothing straightforward about its syncopated rhythms, tricky time signature, ethereal vocals and frenzied synth noodling. Degenhardt's snare-heavy drumming is a masterclass, matched by Dave Ball's nimble bass lines.

This was another song performed on the 1993 tour. In a live video from October 1990, it's part of a medley with 'Depth Charge' and 'Wonderpatch' and features on several live releases including the 2014 *Access All Areas*. The 4:19 'original version' of 'In The Heart of The City' is a bonus track on the 1997 CD reissue of *Guitar Noir* and features Nick Magnus on keyboards.

'Dark as the Grave' 4:38 (Hackett, Friedman)
This is another haunting song with Steve and Friedman improvising tastefully over a looped rhythm track. The colourful keyboard textures of piano and

synth strings are complemented by classical guitar embellishments, although the howling electric sustain gives it a darker edge. The layered, multi-tracked harmonies are sublime as Steve uses the city streets at night as a metaphor for the more sleazy aspects of the human condition.

'Lost in Your Eyes' 4:56 (Hackett, Dave 'Taif' Ball, Julian Colbeck, Hugo Degenhardt)

A song about infatuation for the one you love, this track hits the ground running with its thunderous snare sound and relentless, heavy blues shuffle. It sounds like middle-period Rolling Stones with Steve adopting a lazy, Jagger-esque vocal drawl and letting rip with some mean harmonica soloing. The band had a hand in writing this tune and they're all clearly having a whale of a time playing it.

'Little America' 4:55 (Hackett, Ball, Colbeck, Degenhardt)

This is another full-band offering, although this is a more mellow affair. A cousin of 'Blood on the Rooftops', the subject – channel hopping American TV – was no doubt inspired by endless nights spent in hotel rooms while touring. Degenhardt's crisp drumming boasts inventive fills while Colbeck's piano and Ball's moody bass maintain the steady rhythm. Steve's harmonies are again a delight as are his flights of inspired guitar soloing in the cadenza. It's probably his best playing on the album.

'Like An Arrow' 2:51 (Hackett)

A strummed, single chord acoustic guitar rhythm supports rich keyboard strings, once again from the fingers of Aron Friedman. Steve's monotone singing seems remote and distant, despite the reverb. The lyrics – structured around the repeated song title – are a celebration of the human spirit. The symphonic orchestral coda at 2:15 – again courtesy of Friedman – is one of the most sumptuous on a Hackett record.

'Theatre of Sleep' 3:04 (Hackett)

Another rich keyboard arrangement this time with the sound of plucked strings providing a striking rhythm for this brooding song. In the bridge at 1:50, piano and clarinet combine to create a convincing 1920's smooth jazz waltz. Steve has often used dreams and nightmares as a basis for his lyrics and this is one such song. 'Theatre of Sleep' features Nick Magnus' only keyboard contribution to the album and the track was a later addition following the original CD release in 1993.

'Walking Away From Rainbows' 3:10 (Hackett)

In the sleeve notes for this solo instrumental Steve writes 'Sometimes the afterglow isn't enough and we all must move on'. It's a reference to his

Steve with his favoured Fernandes Les Paul in action at The Summer's End Festival in October 2009. *(Chris Walkden)*

Left: Before plunging into a full-time solo career, Steve tested the water with his 1975 debut album *Voyage of the Acolyte*. (*Charisma*)

Right: On 14 April 1978, just six months after leaving Genesis, Steve released his second album *Please Don't Touch!*. (*Charisma*)

Left: The third album, *Spectral Mornings* released on 26 May 1979, is here shown on LP, CD and cassette. It is still regarded by many as Steve's finest hour - or finest 40 minutes at least. (*Charisma*)

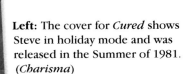

Right: The run of classic albums continues with *Defector*, released on 21 June 1980. (*Charisma*)

Left: The cover for *Cured* shows Steve in holiday mode and was released in the Summer of 1981. (*Charisma*)

Right: The 1983 album *Highly Strung* was Steve's last for Charisma Records, the label he had been with since 1971, when he joined Genesis. (*Charisma*)

Left: *Bay of Kings* is the first of the five mostly acoustic, classical-style albums released by Steve over a period of 25 years.

Right: Steve's eighth album *Till We Have Faces* was his first excursion into world music territory featuring the rhythms of South America. (*Lamborghini Records*)

Left: The second acoustic album *Momentum* includes original compositions in a classical style. (*Start Records*)

Right: *Guitar Noir* - Steve's first rock album in almost nine years - was warmly received by a patient and faithful fanbase. *(Permanent Records)*

Left: Album number eleven *Blues With A Feeling* was another musical departure for Steve which took him back to his 1960s roots. *(Permanent Records)*

Right: In 1996, *Genesis Revisited* gave Steve the opportunity to rework songs originally recorded with his former band between 1971 and 1977. *(Camino)*

Left: Steve's status as one of the UK's finest guitarists has put him on the cover of countless music magazines including *Guitar* in August 1979. *(Geoffrey Feakes)*

Below: Pete Hicks (vocals), John Hackett (guitar) and Nick Magnus (keyboards) in full flow on the German TV series *Musikladen* screened in May 1979.

Above: The author's first Genesis concert with Steve on guitar on the 25 February 1973. It was recorded for the subsequent *Genesis Live* album. *(Geoffrey Feakes)*

Above: Two tickets for Steve Hackett shows from the author's collection. They come from Brussels in November 1980 on the *Defector* tour and from an earlier show in June of the same year at De Montfort Hall in Leicester. *(Geoffrey Feakes)*

Right: Steve performing during the *To Watch the Storms* tour at the Oakwood Centre, Rotherham in October 2003. *(Geoffrey Feakes)*

Left: John, Steve and Roger King returned to Rotherham in March 2005 during the 'Acoustic Trio Tour' where they received a well-deserved ovation. *(Geoffrey Feakes)*

Classic Rock Society in association with Jewels Promotions presents

STEVE HACKETT

OAKWOOD CENTRE
Moorgate Road, Rotherham

Saturday 11th October 2003
Doors: 7:00pm

Tickets: £18 (£16 CRS Subscribers Advance)
Subject To Booking Fee   00039

Classic Rock Society presents

An Acoustic Evening With STEVE HACKETT

OAKWOOD CENTRE
Moorgate Road, Rotherham

Saturday 26th March 2005
Doors: 7:00pm

Tickets: £18 (£15 CRS Members In Advance)
Non member price includes temporary one day CRS membership
Subject To Booking Fee   00012

Above: Steve's shows in Rotherham were staged by the Classic Rock Society which sadly folded in 2019. *(Geoffrey Feakes)*

Left: In 1997, Steve's third classical album *A Midsummer Night's Dream* set William Shakespeare's prose to music with the aid of the Royal Philharmonic Orchestra. (*EMI*)

Right: Although Steve released only five albums in the 1990s, they remain some of his best offerings, including the aptly titled *Darktown*. (*InsideOut*)

STEVEHACKETT FEEDBACK86

ACKETT

Left: Although it was Steve's first release of the new millennium, the songs on *Feedback 86* were recorded in 1986/1987 after his time in GTR. (*Camino*)

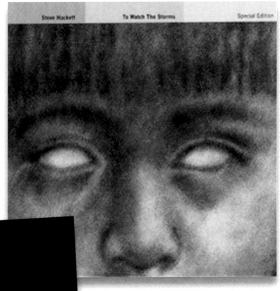

Right: In 2003, *To Watch the Storms* was the first of Steve's albums to be simultaneously released as a standard and expanded 'Special Edition'. (*InsideOut*)

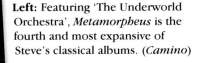

Left: Featuring 'The Underworld Orchestra', *Metamorpheus* is the fourth and most expansive of Steve's classical albums. (*Camino*)

Right: Released in 2006, *Wild Orchids* is a musical travelogue with an eclectic combination of styles. (*Camino*)

Above: Steve performing at the Summer's End Festival in October 2009. *(Chris Walkden)*

Below: Keyboard maestro Roger King at the Summer's End Festival promoting the *Out of the Tunnel's Mouth* album. *(Chris Walkden)*

Above: Gary O'Toole behind the kit at Summer's End. He was Steve's drummer for almost twenty years before departing in 2018. *(Chris Walkden)*

Below: Rob Townsend at Summer's End. His soprano sax gives Steve's and Genesis' songs an extra dimension. *(Chris Walkden)*

Above: Roger King, Nad Sylvan and Steve performing at London's prestigious Royal Albert Hall in October 2013.

Below: The RAH concert was filmed and recorded for the *Genesis Revisited: Live at the Royal Albert Hall* album released in June 2014.

Above: Roger King at London's Eventim Apollo, Hammersmith in November 2019 on the final night of the UK tour.

Below: The Apollo show was released as *Selling England By The Pound & Spectral Mornings: Live At Hammersmith* in September 2020.

Left: Released in 2008, the aptly titled *Tribute* is a homage to classical guitar virtuoso Andrés Segovia. (*Camino*)

Right: Steve's fascination with trains and travel is evident on the twentieth studio album *Out of the Tunnel's Mouth*. (*Wolfwork*)

Left: A firm favourite with fans and critics, *Beyond the Shrouded Horizon* boasted thirteen songs and a further nine on the special edition. (*Wolfwork*)

Right: Steve's second tribute to his former band, *Genesis Revisited II* is a two-CD extravaganza that mostly remains faithful to the source material. (*InsideOut*)

Steve Hackett *Wolflight*

Left: Released in multiple formats in 2015, the cover artwork for *Wolflight* features Steve in the unlikely company of a friendly pack of wolves. (*InsideOut*)

Steve Hackett
The Night Siren

Right: With *The Night Siren* album, Steve fully embraced world music, assisted by a multicultural cast of musicians. (*InsideOut*)

Left: Steve's 25th studio album, the ambitious *At The Edge Of Night*, is arguably his finest since *Spectral Mornings* from 40 years earlier. (*Wolfwork*)

Right: *Under A Mediterranean Sky* mixed solo guitar pieces with other tracks that featured Roger King's lush orchestrations. It was recorded during the Covid 19 restriction in 2020 and released in early 2021. (*InsideOut*)

Left: Released in 2020, *Selling England by the Pound & Spectral Mornings: Live at Hammersmith* features the Steve Hackett band in stunning form. (*InsideOut*)

departure from Genesis in 1977 – 'Afterglow' was the final track on the last album he recorded with the band. It's a haunting piece with gentle nylon guitar underpinned by the Stepp guitar synth providing a soft cushion of strings. It's one of Steve's most tasteful offerings – a track that oozes class.

'Paint Your Picture' 2:58 (Hackett)
A colourful flourish of Spanish guitar sets this evocative song in motion – another solo offering with nylon guitar supported by guitar synth.

'Vampyre With A Healthy Appetite' 5:30 (Hackett)
Very tongue-in-cheek both musically and lyrically, this heavyweight offering harks back to Steve's earlier solo work. Devoid of verses and a chorus, Colbeck, Ball and Degenhardt lay down a relentless main theme, only pausing to allow Steve's processed – and very creepy – vocal interjections. He unleashes manic harmonica and guitar solos along the way and there are engaging percussive and bass solo interludes at 2:17 and 3:44 respectively.

The song was inspired by a newspaper headline that Steve read about the theft of several pints of blood from a hospital in the french quarter of New Orleans. He reset it in the late nineteenth century when Bram Stoker's *Dracula* was published, although here he evokes Anne Rice's Vampire novels, hugely popular in the early 1990s. Unsurprisingly, 'Vampyre with a Healthy Appetite' had staying power as a stage piece and features on *The Tokyo Tapes* live album from 1998. A shorter 4:41 'demo' version is a bonus track on the 1997 CD reissue of *Guitar Noir*.

'Tristesse' 4:02 (Friedman)
Friedman's contribution to *Guitar Noir* is immense and he's also responsible for the closing instrumental. His subtle piano playing anchors the piece, providing the simple – but memorable – central theme while Steve's heavily sustained guitar soars skywards. It is another track that's quite unlike anything he's recorded before, or since. It's dedicated to Roger Weil who wrote the book *Foundations of the Christian Faith*.

Related Tracks
Guitar Noir was remastered in 1997 by Roger King and released with four bonus tracks. These are demo versions of 'Sierra Quemada', 'Take These Pearls', 'In The Heart of the City' and 'Vampyre with a Healthy Appetite' as previously discussed in this chapter.

'Cassandra' 3:42 (Hackett)
This is a hidden track at the end of the American release of *Guitar Noir*. Recorded in 1986, it's a mainstream rock song boasting a ringing guitar hook, a mildly catchy chorus and Brian May of Queen fame on guitar. Steve sings here,

but a longer version with Chris Thompson on lead vocals opens the *Feedback 86* album released in 2000.

'Don't Fall Away From Me' 3:37 (Hackett)

The first of two new songs included on the *The Unauthorised Biography* compilation from 1992. Although from the same session, it's not to be confused with the song 'Don't Fall' on the *Feedback 86* album which is a different, rockier offering. Brian May provides guitar and backing vocals. The circular, twelve-string guitar and piano melody is an absolute delight as are Steve's rich harmonies. It is a contender for the shortlist of Steve's most underrated songs.

'Prayers And Dreams' 4:11 (Hackett)

This is the second new track included on *The Unauthorised Biography* compilation. It's a gentle acoustic guitar instrumental that has a dream-like quality. It was intended for a film about the life of composer Antonio Vivaldi called *Vivaldi, the Red Priest*, which was eventually released in 2009, without Steve's contribution here.

Blues with a Feeling (1994)

Personnel:
Steve Hackett: vocals, guitar, harmonica
Julian Colbeck: keyboards
Doug Sinclair: bass guitar
Hugo Degenhardt: drums
Additional personnel:
Dave 'Taif' Ball: bass guitar on 'Love of Another Kind', 'Way Down South'
Jerry Peal: organ on 'Love of Another Kind'
The Kew Horns on 'Footloose', 'Tombstone Roller', 'Blues With A Feeling':
John Chapman: baritone saxophone
Pete Long: tenor saxophone
John Lee: trumpet
Matt Dunkley: trumpet
Produced by Steve Hackett
Engineered by Jerry Peal, Gerry O'Riordan, Chris Deam
Recorded at: The Basement
Recording date: 1994
Release date: 24 October, 1994
Record label: UK: Kudos Records, USA: Herald
Highest chart places: UK: Did not chart, USA: Did not chart
Running time: 46:30

Steve's eleventh studio album displayed a very different side to his playing.
The title says it all and although these are mostly original compositions, they
pay homage to the music that inspired him in the 1950s and 1960s. It was
a welcome opportunity to return to his teenage roots and cut loose in the
time-honoured fashion of guitarists like B.B. King, Mike Bloomfield and Eric
Clapton, where unfettered soloing took precedence over formal song structure
or experimentation. It's also a showcase for his harmonica talents; as a young
boy, he had started out playing blues-harp eight years before he picked up a
guitar. The album title – taken from one of the tracks – reflects Steve's view
that playing the blues is based on feeling, emotion and self-expression. He also
acknowledges that the electric guitar started out as primarily an instrument of
the blues.

The inclusion of four cover versions was, at that point, rare for a Hackett
album and two songs were written with his then-current band. Although Dave
Ball plays bass on two tracks, he was replaced by Doug Sinclair – who also
toured with Steve – during the recording process. The four-piece horn section
that features on three tracks was also something of an anomaly for Steve. The
album received mixed reviews; many blues purists criticising it for lack of
authenticity while some Hackett fans bemoaned the fact that it was a further
departure from his prog-rock style of the 1970s.

The artwork is a departure from previous covers and is in a more contemporary style. It features a blue-tinged photo of Steve with his name and album title across the middle in plain lettering. The CD booklet, including reissues, wrongly credits the title song to 'Jacobs' – the surname of Little Walter – who performed 'Blues with a Feeling', but didn't write it. The man responsible was drummer, singer and songwriter Robert W. 'Rabon' Tarrant in 1947.

'Born in Chicago' 3:58 (Nick Gravenites)

Steve was inspired by the original recording of this song by the Paul Butterfield Blues Band, released in 1965. The writer, Chicago bluesman Nick Gravenites, now in his 80s, remains active to this day. The title acknowledges that America's third most populated city located on the shores of Lake Michigan – and a great place to visit by the way – is the recognised home of the blues. Steve and his band – mostly the same line-up that recorded *Guitar Noir* – storm their way through this gutsy blues-rocker. I'm no blues expert, but to me, the scorching guitar licks are as good and authentic as any I've heard. That said, it's mostly a platform for Steve's blistering harmonica soloing, influenced by Paul Butterfield who, although a singer and bandleader, was foremostly a blues-harp player.

'The Stumble' 2:55 (Freddie King, Sonny Thompson)

This is a classic blues instrumental that was released as a single by Freddie King in 1962. It's been covered by numerous artists, including the Yardbirds in 1965 and John Mayall and the Bluesbreakers, with Peter Green on guitar, in 1967. It romps along at a lively pace in the style of Status Quo with a rock steady, boogie-woogie riff. Steve's fiery soloing is matched note for note by Doug Sinclair's sterling bass playing. Like Steve, he clearly had an affinity for the genre.

'Love of Another Kind' 4:00 (Steve Hackett)

The album's first original song is another fine showcase for Steve's explosive harmonica and guitar volleys. His double-tracked vocals are excellent as well, as he relates his infatuation with a girl he met on the dancefloor. Engineer Jerry Peal provides some tasteful organ embellishments.

'Way Down South' 4:29 (Hackett)

Steve slows things down a little with this slow blues song. The vocal harmonies are lusher this time around and the instruments are given plenty of space to breathe. The soaring guitar notes cry and sing, and Dave 'Taif' Ball's walking bass line is anything but pedestrian. In the lyrics, the protagonist is returning to a past life to be with his 'southern belle'.

'A Blue Part of Town' 3:04 (Hackett, Julian Colbeck)

The melancholic mood continues with this aptly titled instrumental, which has a sultry, late-night vibe. Backed solely by Colbeck's brooding electric piano, it's a showcase for Steve's solo harmonica talents. You really have to hear this track to appreciate just how good a harp player he is, ringing every last shred of emotion from the instrument.

'Footloose' 2:30 (Hackett)

This is another appropriately-titled instrumental as Steve and the band return to high octane, rhythm and blues territory. It has nothing to do with the similarly titled 1984 hit song and film, but the track motors along at a manic pace, driven by a relentless rhythm where once again, Sinclair's articulate bass playing stands out. Steve's guitar goes into overdrive and the addition of the four-piece horn section and piano give the track an authentic big band swing.

'Tombstone Roller' 5:18 (Hackett)

Suitably, the longest track on the album is also its most eclectic offering. To begin with, harmonica is once again front and centre, while Hugo Degenhardt's propulsive drumming keeps things moving at an energetic pace. For his heavily-processed vocal, Steve affects an American deep south drawl. The call and response interplay between the vocal and instrumental sections is especially reminiscent of Led Zeppelin's 'Black Dog', while the lengthy instrumental coda that begins at 2:21 soars to grandiose heights with guitar volleys punctuated by roaring keyboards and horns. The words are suitably optimistic, suggesting that if a man tries hard enough, he can return from the grave.

'Blues with a Feeling' 4:23 (Rabon Tarrant)

Although Chicago blues-harp player Little Walter popularised this song in 1953, Steve was inspired by a version on the eponymous 1965 debut album by *The Paul Butterfield Blues Band*. It's a slow blues shuffle, featuring superb harmonica soling and that most famous of walking blues patterns. Steve's performance is assured and both his singing and guitar playing bring Eric Clapton to mind who, in turn, was inspired by bluesman Big Bill Broonzy. The middle-eight at 3:42 adds an authentic touch of 1950s style rock and roll to the mix.

'Big Dallas Sky' 4:48 (Hackett, Colbeck, Doug Sinclair, Hugo Degenhardt)

A full band composition, this is in a more mainstream rock vein. The song opens with a layering of mellow synths and guitar with Steve's sinister, Lou Reed-style half-spoken, half-sung vocal again evoking the American south. In contrast, the soaring guitar flights, lively piano fills and circular, skipping rhythm are supremely melodic. It's not the blues, but it is one of the album's most accessible offerings. The lyrics tell of a man's search across the wide-open spaces of Texas for his lost love.

'The 13th Floor' 3:29 (Hackett)

In contrast, this is a loose jam. Colbeck's honky-tonk piano accompanies Steve's histrionic, heavy-blues inflected guitar-shredding complete with dive-bombing sustain at 2:50. Drums and bass are conspicuously absent, giving the track a rough demo feel.

'So Many Roads' 3:16 (Marshall Paul)

Originally titled 'So Many Roads, So Many Trains', American blues guitarist Otis Rush released the first version of this song in 1960. It was covered by John Mayall's Bluesbreakers featuring Peter Green in 1966 and The Climax Blues Band in 1969. Again, we're in slow blues territory with Steve's falsetto vocal at the beginning sounding almost like a female balladeer. He reverts to his normal tenor for the rest of the song. In fact, he gives one of his most soulful vocal performances, matched by some classy guitar fills and solos.

'Solid Ground' 4:28 (Hackett, Colbeck, Sinclair, Degenhardt)

Another full band arrangement, the central harmonica riff was extracted from the 1986 song 'Don't Fall' which did not see the light of day until 2000 on the *Feedback 86* album. It's an unashamed, full-blooded blues-rocker with a larynx shredding vocal from Steve as he recalls an uneasy relationship. The extended instrumental playout that weighs in at 2:40 provides ample space for guitar improvisation heavy on the sustain, although the rhythm section remains rock solid.

Related Tracks

The reissue by Esoteric Recordings in June 2016 includes two bonus tracks that, unusually, were newly written and recorded for the reissue. On both tracks, Steve is backed by Roger King on keyboards who also remastered the new version. An enhanced reissue in America in 2003 by InsideOut Music includes the 6:32 video *Tokyo '96* but no bonus tracks. Like several of Steve's other albums, *Blues with a Feeling* has also been reissued in the UK and other regions with MP3 files of previously-available studio and live material. Look out for the words 'This is an enhanced CD – please put it in your computer'.

'On Cemetery Road' 3:07 (Steve Hackett, Jo Hackett)

Clearly a more recent recording, this song is far removed from the sound and style of the 1994 recordings with scarcely a hint of blues. King provides the bouncing 4/4 rhythm, allowing Steve's restrained vocals and guitar soloing to take centre stage. The song is about a young hopeful who makes a blood pact with the devil but finds that his new powers come at a price.

'Patch of Blue' 4:37 (Steve Hackett)

This track is closer to the spirit of the original album, although in a more modern blues-rock vein. According to Steve's liner notes, the title comes from the line '...that little patch of blue which prisoners call the sky' in Oscar Wilde's 1897 poem 'The Ballad of Reading Gaol'. However, Wilde actually wrote '...that little *tent of blue* which prisoners call the sky'. But enough of my nitpicking, this is an agreeable instrumental that really swings with aggressive guitar soloing underpinned by King's organ.

Genesis Revisited (1996/1997)

Personnel:

Steve Hackett: guitar, vocals, harmonica, percussion, backing vocals, orchestration

John Wetton: vocals on 'Watcher of the Skies'; vocals, bass on 'Firth of Fifth'

Paul Carrack: vocals on 'Déjà Vu', 'Your Own Special Way'

Colin Blunstone: vocals on 'For Absent Friends'

John Hackett: flute on 'The Fountain of Salmacis'

Will Bates: saxophone on 'Dance on a Volcano', 'Waiting Room Only', 'I Know What I Like'

Ian McDonald: saxophone, flute on 'Los Endos'

'Spats' King: vibes on 'I Know What I Like'

Julian Colbeck: keyboards on 'Watcher of the Skies', 'Dance on a Volcano', 'The Fountain of Salmacis'

Roger King: keyboards, orchestration, programming, additional programming

Ben Fenner: keyboards, orchestration, programming, additional programming

Nick Magnus: keyboards, programming on 'Valley of the Kings'

Jerry Peal: keyboards, programming on 'Valley of the Kings'

Aron Friedman: orchestration on 'For Absent Friends'; orchestration, keyboards, programming on 'Your Own Special Way'; keyboards, piano on 'I Know What I Like'

Tony Levin: bass on 'Watcher of the Skies'

Alphonso Johnson: bass on 'Dance on a Volcano', 'The Fountain of Salmacis'

Pino Palladino: bass on 'Déjà Vu', 'Los Endos'

Bill Bruford: drums on 'Watcher of the Skies'; drums, percussion on 'Firth of Fifth'

Chester Thompson: drums on 'Dance on a Volcano', 'The Fountain of Salmacis'; additional drums on 'Los Endos'

Hugo Degenhardt: drums on 'Valley of the Kings', 'Déjà Vu', 'Waiting Room Only', 'Los Endos'

Tarquin Bombast: drums on 'I Know What I Like'

Richard Macphail, Jeanne Downs & Richard Wayler: backing vocals on 'Your Own Special Way'

The Sanchez/Montoya Chorale on 'Déjà Vu', 'Waiting Room Only'

Anton De Bruck: chorale director

Royal Philharmonic Orchestra

Matt Dunkley: Orchestra arranger, conductor

Produced by Steve Hackett

Engineered by Roger King, Ben Fenner, Jerry Peal, Gerry O'Riordan

Recorded at: The Basement, Westside, Matrix, RG Jones and The Farm, Nashville

Recording date: 1996 – 1997

Release date: 1996/1997

Record label: UK: Reef Recordings, USA: Guardian Records

Highest chart places: UK: 95, USA: Did not chart

Running time: 76:43

Another self-explanatory title, this is Steve's first excursion into the back catalogue of the band he left nineteen years earlier. And he didn't travel alone; rarely has there been such an impressive line-up of singers and musicians on one album. Steve's trip down memory lane dips into the six albums recorded during his tenure with Genesis, which was arguably their most creative period. He also took the opportunity to include one of his own songs – or two on the Japanese version – for the benefit of Genesis fans who may have otherwise been out of touch with his current work. Ironically, when Steve recorded the album, Genesis were in limbo. Phil Collins departed In March 1996 and Tony Banks and Mike Rutherford had yet to find a replacement.

Recording sessions began on 6 April 1996 with Steve initially working with ex-Genesis touring drummers, Bill Bruford and Chester Thompson. It was Steve's intention to breathe new life into the material motivated by the belief that the original studio recordings paled in comparison with live performances. While some songs remain faithful to the originals, others were deconstructed and re-assembled and the Royal Philharmonic Orchestra were on hand to add weight to these new recordings.

As surprising as it may seem now, Steve struggled to secure a record deal and initially, the album was released in Japan only, in August 1996. Ten days of rehearsals at the beginning of December prepared Steve and his 'special guests' John Wetton, Chester Thompson, Ian McDonald and Julian Colbeck for a mini-tour of Japan to promote the album. It was a resounding success and two shows in Tokyo on 16 and 17 December were filmed and later released as *The Tokyo Tapes* on CD, VHS and DVD.

Genesis Revisited was released in the UK and other regions outside Japan on 22 September, 1997. Steve's solo track 'Riding the Colossus', which is on the Japanese version of the album, was replaced with a new recording of 'Los Endos'. *Genesis Revisited* marked Steve's return to the UK chart for the first time since *Till We Have Faces* thirteen years earlier (when, from 4 October 1997, it lingered for just one week). The reaction from fans was mixed, especially those familiar with the Genesis originals. Many, including myself, were surprised by some of the song selections but welcomed the mostly-excellent individual performances.

The cover artwork is disappointing, especially the heavy-handed symbolism. It depicts Adam and Eve – presumably representing Genesis the band – being blasted by a fleet of flying saucers, no doubt piloted by Hackett and his new crew. The American release features the same artwork with the additional 'Watcher of the Skies' title at the start.

'Watcher of the Skies' 8:40 (Tony Banks, Phil Collins, Peter Gabriel, Steve Hackett, Mike Rutherford)

An inspired opener, this famous track also launched the 1972 *Foxtrot* album, *Genesis Live* and the 1972-1974 Genesis shows. The track always provided a gothic atmosphere in large venues where it would virtually shake the foundations. Julian Colbeck's Mellotron samples played on a Korg 01/W synth faithfully reproduce the dense wall of sound opening chords. Ironically, given that the Mellotron is essentially an orchestra substitute, here the Royal Philharmonic plays second fiddle (if you excuse the pun). During the song section, which is in 6/4 time, John Wetton does a credible job with the words which were influenced by Arthur C. Clarke's sci-fi novel *Childhood's End.* In addition to Wetton, Bill Bruford and Tony Levin are on drums and bass respectively, giving the recording a strong King Crimson connection.

'Dance on a Volcano' 7:28 (Banks, Collins, Hackett, Rutherford)

This, of course, is the opening song from *A Trick of the Tail,* one of the author's favourite albums. Here it does seem to take an age to get going, opening with random chords before the fanfare proper kicks in at 1:33. With a compelling riff, it's another song that works superbly live. The dynamic rhythm combination of Chester Thompson and Alphonso Johnson performs the tricky rhythm which is in 7/8 time to perfection and although you can't dance to it, the track really swings. Even though the fast and furious end section – which Steve wrote – is a challenge to play live, he still enjoys performing the song to this day. His deep, processed vocal does take some getting used to, however.

'Valley of the Kings' 6:30 (Jerry Peal, Hackett)

Although the Valley of the Kings is 650 kilometres due south of Cairo, the building of the great pyramids inspired this epic sounding instrumental, a worthy, non-Genesis addition to the album. It's another track that takes a while to warm-up, but it's worth the wait. Hugo Degenhardt's stop-start drum stomp is worthy of John Bonham, while Steve's guitar screams and cries over the top. Nick Magnus is responsible for the exotic middle-eastern-flavoured keyboard arrangement. The theme came to Steve in a surreal dream about ancient Egypt, and the music was designed to capture the spirit of that time. The fact that the piece develops with Genesis-style chords validates its inclusion here.

'Déjà Vu' 5:55 (Gabriel, Hackett)

Peter Gabriel brought the barebones of this song to the 1973 *Selling England by the Pound* sessions, but it was never finished or recorded. Steve liked the chords and the ending, so with Peter's permission, he completed the song for this album. He also asked the former Genesis frontman if he would sing it, but Gabriel declined. The superb Paul Carrack is a more than capable substitute, giving a heart-rending performance of this bittersweet ballad. The orchestra strings and woodwind sound suitably sumptuous and the ringing guitar refrain at 2:09 is to die for. It's a track that holds its own against anything else on the album and the haunting nylon guitar theme towards the end is the icing on the cake. When Steve toured *Selling England by the Pound* in its entirety in 2019, this song was played as a bonus.

'Firth of Fifth' 9:40 (Banks, Collins, Gabriel, Hackett, Rutherford)
This is the first of two songs from *Selling England by the Pound,* Steve's favourite Genesis album. It's also – unsurprisingly – one of his favourite Tony Banks compositions and it's his most played song on stage. He takes one or two liberties with this classic – particularly the keyboard parts – which threaten to mar an otherwise fine version. The introduction forsakes piano for a tame glockenspiel arrangement while Banks' soaring ARP synth solo is replaced by random stabs from the orchestra that sound totally out of place. Wetton's vocal doesn't quite convey the same stately gravitas as Gabriel's original, but he would nonetheless make this song his own when performing it regularly with Steve. The iconic guitar solo, complete with long sustain, is as you would expect, all present and correct. The original Genesis version featured three separate guitar takes played back together and live it always brought the house down and remains a regular part of Steve's repertoire.

'For Absent Friends' 3:02 (Banks, Collins, Gabriel, Hackett, Rutherford)
This is the delightful song from the 1971 *Nursery Cryme* album, Steve's debut recording with Genesis. Written by the two new recruits Steve and Phil Collins, the original version was the drummer's first lead vocal for the band. Here, ex-Zombies frontman Colin Blunstone provides an equally sensitive vocal and the tempo, which is slowed to Walz time, suits his wistful style perfectly. The gorgeous, baroque orchestral arrangement, with sweet strings and woodwind, gives it that extra lift resulting in one of the album's best interpretations.

'Your Own Special Way' 4:19 (Rutherford)
Originally on the *Wind & Wuthering* album, this was Genesis' most radio-friendly song up to that point and their first to enter the American singles chart. Rutherford dedicated the song to his wife Angie and Steve rates it as one of Mike's most beautiful. Here, it's given a late-night, cocktail bar vibe but is none the worse for that. It features another stunning interpretation by Paul Carrack with electric piano and rich keyboard orchestrations from Aron Friedman. The vocal backing is strong, while the Royal Philharmonic serenades serenely in the background and Steve lets fly with a soaring solo at 2:48. It was released as a single in 1998 to promote *Genesis Revisited,* but it failed to match the success of the original.

'The Fountain of Salmacis' 9:54 (Banks, Collins, Gabriel, Hackett, Rutherford)
Another song from *Nursery Cryme,* this mini-epic, with its poetic lyrics based on Greek mythology, closed that album. It was one of the first tracks Steve recorded with Genesis and was reworked from a previous, uncompleted

song that was written prior to his arrival. He was, however, responsible for the closing guitar solo. He strays from the original by opening with a classical guitar solo before the familiar organ and Mellotron crescendos that epitomise early Genesis. Like their version, this goes for the full cinematic, widescreen approach with Alphonso Johnson's throbbing bassline making its presence felt superbly. The frantic, bolero instrumental sequence at the midway point remains the best section and the orchestra add their weight to create a suitably epic sound. Steve delivers the vocals nicely before playing the track out with his showboating solo.

'Waiting Room Only' 6:53 (Hackett, Roger King)
Steve had unhappy memories of *The Lamb Lies Down on Broadway* era, which is perhaps why it's barely represented here. Although the title song was reportedly rehearsed for the album, this track is as close as it gets in the end, a loose variation on the instrumental 'The Waiting Room'. The original was born from a jam session during rehearsals for *The Lamb* and underwent numerous changes when performed live. Here, Steve attempts to recapture the same spontaneity. Whereas Tony Banks utilised a Mellotron choir on 'The Waiting Room', here the Sanchez/Montoya Chorale provide the haunting vocals while Roger King adds orchestrated rasps and blasts. The second half really swings – sounding like a Danny Elfman film score – with Steve rocking out with both guitar and harmonica.

'I Know What I Like (In Your Wardrobe)' 5:37 (Banks, Collins, Gabriel, Hackett, Rutherford)
When Steve began touring in October 1978, this – along with the solo guitar piece 'Horizons' – was the only Genesis song in his solo repertoire. He regularly played it as an encore, so its inclusion here is hardly surprising. Based on a guitar riff, the song originated from Steve and Phil Collins and was initially rejected by Genesis, but went on to become their first hit single, reaching number 21 in the UK chart in April 1974. Steve plays fast and loose with this interpretation, slowing it down to a laid back, jazz-swing tempo. The treatment is suitably carefree, and during the lengthy midsection, he introduces the various instruments – *Tubular Bells* style – with a mock American accent. It's a lighthearted romp although some listeners may miss the singalong zest of the Genesis version.

'Los Endos' 8:51 (Banks, Collins, Hackett, Rutherford)
This is, of course, the closing instrumental from the 1976 *A Trick of the Tail* album and Genesis' set closer and encore of choice for several years thereafter. This version was recorded after the Japanese release of *Genesis Revisited* and features King Crimson founding member Ian McDonald on saxophone and flute. Steve always viewed this as Genesis' answer to Santana and here the Latin rhythms – in which he had become well versed following his trips to

Brazil – are emphasised. The Pino Palladino and Hugo Degenhardt rhythm section really cooks and the frantic Crimson-style soloing featuring Steve, Ian McDonald and Roger King is a joy. Overall, the piece has a punchy, live sound making it probably the most successful interpretation here. The massed drums in the finale – with Chester Thompson adding his rhythmic muscle – are stunning.

Related Tracks
'Riding The Colossus' 3:30 (Hackett)
The Japanese version of *Genesis Revisited* has a different track sequencing and includes this non-Genesis instrumental. It was replaced with 'Los Endos' for later releases elsewhere including the UK. It's one of Steve's most tuneful compositions and rivals the best of his work from the 1970s. The title is taken from the twin wooden roller coaster ride in Valencia, California and the tone is suitably exhilarating with a stirring, cut glass guitar theme. Unsurprisingly, it was a stage favourite and is included on *The Tokyo Tapes* live CD and DVD. A different arrangement had previously appeared on the 1992 live album *Time Lapse* under the title 'Depth Charge'.

'Firewall' 4:41 (Hackett)
Both this instrumental and 'The Dealer' were recorded around the time of the *Genesis Revisited* sessions and were bonus tracks on the 1998 *The Tokyo Tapes* double CD. They both feature Steve on guitar and Aron Friedman on keyboards and programming. Curiously, the synths and synthetic drum sounds give the piece a dated 1980s feel, but the sizzling guitar lines make it a worthwhile venture. It could have made suitable material for the soundtrack to an action thriller.

'The Dealer' 4:23 (Hackett)
This has a more laid back, mid-tempo groove and like 'Riding The Colossus', boasts a strong melody on which the rest of the track hangs. The musicianship of Steve and Aron is faultless as they indulge in some welcome, jazzy instrumental exchanges.

A Midsummer Night's Dream (1997)

Personnel:
Steve Hackett: classical guitar, arrangements
Roger King: St. Simon Zelotes church organ on 'Celebration', arrangements
John Hackett: flute on 'Between The Cold Moon & The Earth', 'Peaseblossom, Cobweb, Moth & Mustardseed', 'The Lunatic, The Lover & The Poet'
Matt Dunkley: orchestrations, conductor
The Royal Philharmonic Orchestra
Produced by Steve Hackett
Recorded and mixed by Roger King
Recorded at: Air Studios, Lyndhurst Hall, London & St. Simon Zelotes, Chelsea, London
Recording date: 1996 – 1997
Release date: 1 April 1997
Record label: UK: EMI/Camino Classics, USA: Angel Records
Highest chart places: UK: Did not chart, USA: Did not chart
Running time: 62:32

Having worked with the Royal Philharmonic on *Genesis Revisited*, Steve re-engaged the orchestra for his third classical album. As the title suggests, it's based on William Shakespeare's popular late sixteenth-century play. The compositions are all original, owing nothing to Felix Mendelssohn's nineteenth-century musical adaptation. It started out as a three-part suite comprising 'By Paved Fountain', 'Titania' and 'Set Your Heart At Rest', which was eventually expanded to eighteen parts to do the play full justice. It's Steve's first full concept since 1975's *Voyage of the Acolyte* and each track provides a leitmotif for the various characters and scenes in the play. An expansive, lyrical and romantic story set in Ancient Greece, it was, in Steve's mind, the ideal subject for a musical adaptation combining classical guitar and a full orchestra. The latter was recorded at London's Air Studios – which contains one of the world's largest rooms for orchestral recording – under the direction of Steve's cousin Matt Dunkley who fulfilled similar duties on *Genesis Revisited*.

It was also keyboardist, arranger and engineer Roger King's second album with Steve, inheriting roles previously occupied by John Acock, Nick Magnus and Julian Colbeck. King had previously worked for Island Music, recording several of their mainstream acts. Additionally, John Hackett plays flute on three tracks. The combination of guitar and orchestra is superbly realised, giving the album a timeless quality and it was Steve's most enthusiastically received album for several years, appealing to both fans and critics alike. Although it missed out on the main UK album chart, it did reach the top ten of the classical chart.

That same year, Steve found himself involved with Genesis live recordings for the first time since the mixing of *Seconds Out* twenty years earlier. A version of *The Lamb Lies Down on Broadway* recorded at Los Angeles' Shrine Auditorium on 24 January 1975 was being dusted down for the 4 CD *Genesis Archive 1967–75*. Because of his hand injury and subsequent operation in 1974 prior to *The Lamb* tour, Steve's playing had not been at its best during the American leg. He found out about the proposed box-set through Peter Gabriel and although he was annoyed that he hadn't been invited to participate, he re-recorded some of the guitar parts, later commenting that he preferred the live version to the studio original.

In 1996, several paintings were produced for *A Midsummer Night's Dream,* two of which were used for the cover in different regions. The first, titled 'Titania Awakes', features a nude image of Titania the queen of the fairies while the second, 'Within This Wood', depicts a winged fairy. Although the album is purely instrumental, the notes in the CD booklet for each track give a detailed description of the corresponding scene in the play with Shakespeare's verse also quoted.

'The Palace Of Theseus' 2:47 (Steve Hackett)
The play – and the album – opens in the residence of the Duke of Athens where Theseus is preparing for his pending wedding to Hippolyta, Queen of the Amazons. Despite the play's Greek setting, Steve's nylon guitar introduction has a distinctly Spanish flavour with rapid, flamenco-style fingering. The orchestra makes a brief appearance at 1:07 and again at 1:47 before returning in earnest at 2:13 for the exuberant, string-driven coda. The shadow of Joaquin Rodrigo's 'Concierto de Aranjuez' looms large over this piece.

'A Form In Wax' 4:40 (Hackett)
Theseus counsels Hernia, one of the young lovers in the play, advising that her dictatorial father Egeus has the power to shape her future as if she was 'a form in wax'. The orchestra opens this track with a lush but melancholic theme for strings. Compared with the previous piece, Steve's playing is more reticent at first, but he kicks up his heels for the glorious second part where he's joined by the orchestra for a rapturous melody.

'By Paved Fountain' 2:00 (Hackett)
This is a reference to one of the idyllic, pastoral settings 'by paved fountain or by rushy brook' where Theseus and Titania the Fairy Queen meet. It's a beautifully understated solo guitar exercise in scene-setting. Steve's rippling note clusters have a floating, dream-like quality.

'Titania' 2:23 (Hackett)
A flighty leitmotif for the Fairy Queen who has come to the forest outside Athens with Oberon, the Fairy King. Steve's expressive solo guitar flits,

glides and darts with a sweet, playful theme at its core, as Titania asserts her intention to attend Theseus' wedding.

'Set Your Heart At Rest' 3:31 (Hackett)

The title is a lighthearted retort from Titania to a troubled Oberon. A tranquil guitar piece from Steve with a restrained, but memorable, melody. Absent from the previous two tracks, the orchestra strings and woodwind return at 3:00 for the sumptuous finale, bringing to mind Ennio Morricone's splendid 1986 film score for *The Mission*.

'Oberon' 2:31 (Hackett)

A character study focusing on the Fairy King and the good-natured battle of wills with his estranged Queen. Steve's lively playing almost dances out of the speakers with a barely contained, gleeful spring in its step.

'Within This Wood' 2:36 (Hackett)

A revengeful Oberon conspires to play his magic flower trick on Titania. The guitar builds from hesitant, low key beginnings, with dexterous picking, into a jaunty frolic. It captures the image of an oblivious Titania who is playing happily in the woods.

'In The Beached Margent Of The Sea' 2:38 (Hackett, Roger King)

With the windswept sea as a backdrop, Titania meets with Theseus. The full might of the Royal Philharmonic convey the sweeping grandeur of this piece, complimented by Steve's rippling guitar chords. It is one of the album's most satisfyingly dramatic pieces, that ends all too soon.

'Between The Cold Moon & The Earth' 2:44 (Hackett)

Oberon consorts with his jester Puck in the mischievous trick he has planned for Titania. The rich, stately splendour of the orchestra conveys Oberon's authority, while Steve's playful guitar chords hint at his roguish intent. The piece has another sumptuous melody and is the first of three tracks that feature John Hackett on flute.

'Puck' 1:53 (Hackett)

The 'shrewd and knavish sprite' Robin 'Puck' Goodfellow is confronted by one of Titania's fairies. Appropriately, Steve's guitar sends a flurry of notes cascading in all directions. It boasts some of his most rapid and complex playing on the album but remains joyfully zestful throughout.

'Helena' 4:21 (Hackett)

The orchestra maintains a majestic dignity for the character of Helena, who is desperately in love with Demetrius. Guitar similarly conveys an air of solemn romanticism with another fine melody.

'Peaseblossom, Cobweb, Moth & Mustardseed' 4:28 (Hackett)
The evocative title refers to the four fairies who dutifully attend to Titania after she falls prey to Oberon's devious prank. John's pastoral flute provides the intro leaving Steve's guitar to sketch the distinctive personality of each fairy. Frantic chords contrast with elements of serene calm.

'Mountains Turned Into Clouds' 4:36 (Hackett)
Another evocative line from the Bard inspired this majestic piece which features the Royal Philharmonic at their awe-inspiring best. The melody is stunning, evoking the romanticism of Ralph Vaughan Williams. Despite this being the only track on the album not to feature guitar, along with the penultimate piece 'Celebration', it remains my favourite.

'The Lunatic, The Lover & The Poet' 4:14 (Hackett)
Another character study, this time describing those who have gathered in the Palace of Theseus for what has now become a triple marriage ceremony. In keeping with the occasion, the orchestra strings and John Hackett's flute convey a courtly elegance in the classical baroque style. Steve's playful guitar melody – delightful as it is – owes a clear debt to Johann Sebastian Bach's 'Jesu, Joy Of Man's Desiring'.

'Starlight' 4:48 (Hackett)
Described by Theseus as 'evening's lazy time'. Strings and woodwind remain respectfully discrete as Steve gracefully picks his way through another gorgeous melody. The stately finale after the orchestra enters at 3:41 brings to mind the Regency period film scores of Patrick Doyle, one of the author's favourite composers.

'Lysander & Demetrius' 2:45 (Hackett)
There is a moment of rivalry between the play's two young suitors although, as Puck reflects, all will work out well in the end. Following the lyrical flute and strings intro, Steve once again returns to the sprightly Spanish style for which he clearly has an affection. It's another masterclass in classical guitar playing on an album overflowing with virtuoso performances.

'Celebration' 6:15 (Hackett)
Following the group ceremony with Theseus married to Hippolyta, Lysander to Hermia and Demetrius to Helena, the celebrations begin. For many fans of the album, this is the standout track, as well as the longest. Steve's spirited playing conveys the joyful mood of the occasion, punctuated by Roger King's celestial organ stabs. The organ was recorded at the church of St. Simon Zelotes in Chelsea, London. The orchestra is in a jubilant mood with fanfare-like trumpets, soaring strings and playful woodwind and the call and response

interplay between organ and trumpets is inspired. A moment of quiet reflection closes the track as a reconciled Titania and Oberon bless the beds of the newlyweds.

'All Is Mended' 3:13 (Hackett)

After all the other characters depart, Puck reflects that the upheaval and misdemeanours that have permeated the convoluted plot have been put right. He also suggests to the play's audience that it may have all been a dream. Appropriately, Steve plays out with a reflective nylon guitar lament, bringing things to a serene conclusion.

Related Tracks

Understandably, given the self-contained subject, there were no bonus tracks on subsequent reissues.

Darktown (1999)

Personnel:
Steve Hackett: guitar, harmonica, piano, strings, violin, vocals, choir, chorus, twelve-string guitar, woodwind, rainstick, sequencing, orchestration, twelve-string bass guitar, nylon guitar
Roger King: keyboards, bass, drums, flageolet, Mellotron
Julian Colbeck: keyboards on 'Darktown'
Hugo Degenhardt: drums on 'Rise Again'
Jim Diamond: vocals on 'Days of Long Ago'
Ben Fenner: strings, children choir arrangement on 'The Golden Age of Steam', Mellotron, organ, DX7 synth on 'Twice Around the Sun'
Aron Friedman: piano, keyboards on 'Rise Again'
John Hackett: flute, pan pipes on 'Dreaming with Open Eyes'
Ian McDonald: saxophone on 'Darktown'
Jerry Peal: strings, bells on 'The Golden Age of Steam', strings, bass, keyboards on 'Dreaming with Open Eyes'
Doug Sinclair: bass on 'Omega Metallicus', fretless bass on 'Twice Around the Sun'
Billy Budis: cello on 'Days of Long Ago', bass on 'Rise Again'
John Wetton: bass samples on 'In Memoriam'
Jamie McKenna & Mae McKenna: end choir on 'The Golden Age of Steam'
Produced by Steve Hackett
Recorded and mixed by: Roger King, Richard Buckland, Ben Fenner, Jerry Pearl, Billy Budis
Recording date: 1996 – 1998
Release date: 4 May 1999
Record label: UK & Europe: Camino Records
Highest chart places: UK: 156, USA: Did not chart
Running time: 56:33

Darktown is one of Steve's most personal albums, which he describes as 'autobiographical' in the sleeve notes. It's also a particular favourite of this author. It certainly deserved greater success than it achieved at the time. That said, it was generally well-received by a loyal fanbase who regarded it as a return to the progressive rock form of the 1970s. Mainstream critics, by this time, had become mostly dismissive of his albums. Like all his best work, there is a fine balance between stirring instrumentals and haunting songs and despite the sombre tone, the album exudes a good deal of charm. Only the title song and the closing track 'In Memoriam' would become established in Steve's live repertoire.

 Once again, Steve elected to record with a long list of guests, although these were becoming familiar names rather than random session musicians. The only downside is the reliance on programmed rhythms, samples and loops, a sign of the times, but a disappointment nonetheless. With several keyboardists involved, most notably Roger King, the album was Julian Colbeck's swansong, having performed and recorded with Steve since 1989. His contributions are restricted to one piece – the title track – which also includes King.

That same year, the Genesis class of '74 reconvened to record 'The Carpet Crawlers 1999' for *Turn It On Again: The Hits*. Steve later regretted his involvement and was critical of Trevor Horn's production on the re-recording and the compilation in general, declaring that it was 'very guitar light'. This feeling is hardly surprising, given that he – and Peter Gabriel – feature on only two of the eighteen tracks. Steve's frustration is understandable, indeed on the 1977 *Seconds Out* live album, his guitar is similarly low in the mix.

The sombre artwork for *Darktown* by Harry and Lippa Pearce is a departure from previous releases. Shadowy, black and white photos taken in an overgrown cemetery appear on the front and back of the CD slipcase and booklet. Steve's detailed liner notes provide a welcome insight into the story behind each track, although, unfortunately, there is no information as to when and where each was recorded.

'Omega Metallicus' 3:48 (Steve Hackett)

The muscular, opening instrumental certainly lives up to its title. Doug Sinclair's funky, slapped-bass riff drives the track as Steve and Roger King let fly with all manner of shrieking guitar improvisations, keyboard effects and percussive loops. As Steve points out in the liner notes, his trusty Fernandes Les Paul is responsible for the piercing sustain which at 3:17, seems to go on forever. There's even a strummed acoustic guitar chord in there somewhere.

'Darktown' 4:59 (Hackett)

The title song is a critique of certain, disreputable factions of the British education system who abuse their power over children. Judging, by his liner notes, Steve – an ex-grammar schoolboy – is speaking from the viewpoint of a former victim. Opening with a swaying guitar riff, his heavily processed vocal is suitably dark and sinister – like something out of a horror film. Roger King and Julian Colbeck are jointly responsible for the monumental and moody orchestral backdrop, while the improvised saxophone screams are courtesy of ex-King Crimson maestro Ian McDonald. 'Darktown' is one of the few songs from the album to be performed in concert and remained a set-list regular, up until 2004 at least.

'Man Overboard' 4:17 (Hackett)

A nylon guitar motif backed by strummed twelve-string provides the tranquil intro to this piece. Steve's mellow vocal refrain features lush, muli-tracked harmonies – shades of 10cc's 'I'm Not In Love' – supported by acoustic guitar and light percussion. The symphonic keyboard bridge at 2:02 is heavenly, as is the rich choral backing which Steve describes as 'The Siedlaczek Choir'. He wrote this song while on holiday in Bermuda and the words reflect on the times when we should all slow down and take things easy with deeply evocative lines like 'we'll sit and watch the sun go down'.

'The Golden Age of Steam' 4:09 (Hackett)

A man who likes to travel, this song is one of many that reveal Steve's fascination with trains. The song's subject goes deeper than that, however. Inspired by *The Diary of Anne Frank*, it's the fictionalised story of a young boy who spies for the Nazis in order to survive during world war two. Although it wasn't performed with any regularity following the album, it was resurrected for the 2010 tour in support of the *Out of the Tunnel's Mouth* album.

Steve's close-miked vocals tell the story supported by a rhythmic orchestral backdrop put together by the multi-talented Ben Fenner, using samples. The song's driving, march-like rhythm made Steve think of a steam train in motion. The marching flutes and mandolin-like guitar sequence at 1:43 is superb, while various vocal effects, including a chorus of marching soldiers, a genuine news commentary from the period and a children's choir are used to create the atmosphere of the wartime setting. The end result is one of Steve's most ambitious tracks to date.

'Days of Long Ago' 3:23 (Jim Diamond, Hackett)

This is a haunting ballad that was co-written with the song's singer, Jim Diamond. It's the most unashamedly romantic song on a Hackett album since 'Hoping Love Will Last' in 1978. It also provides a warm-glow respite from the darkness that pervades a good deal of the album. Diamond was responsible for the lyrics which, judging by the copyright, date back to 1991. His name is appropriate given his distinctive, cut-glass voice that was responsible for three top-five UK hits during the 1980s. Call me on old softy, but I adore this song, one of my all-time favourites on any of Steve's albums. From the bittersweet verses to the heartbreaking chorus – especially when augmented by strings – it's perfection. The harp-like acoustic guitar bridge at 2:11 is the icing on the cake. 'Days of Long Ago' was released as a promo single but sadly failed to attract the same airplay that Diamond had enjoyed the previous decade, despite his name appearing on the sleeve.

'Dreaming with Open Eyes' 6:54 (Hackett)

This piece was described by Steve as a car journey set to music. The song reflects on how a person – lulled by the car's mechanical rhythms – daydreams and thinks of far off or imaginary places while driving and listening to the radio. Steve's three-part harmonies are backed by a stark shuffle rhythm – produced by a slapped and then slowed down nylon guitar. One can almost visualise the sun's rays bouncing off the windscreen as he drives past a tree-lined setting. The extended, jazzy instrumental bridge at 2:11 is sublime and features impromptu piano, acoustic guitar, and vibes. The pan pipes and flute are courtesy of brother John and the backwards orchestral outro is inspired.

'Twice Around the Sun' 7:15 (Hackett)

This is a stunning instrumental and one of Steve's best guitar workouts since 'Spectral Mornings' from twenty years earlier. The strong melody and arrangement embody everything good about his music, even though the stop-start, walking pace bears more than a passing resemblance to 'Tommy' by Focus – a tune covered by Steve in the noughties. There is even a hint of Gary Moore's 'Parisienne Walkways'.

The track is awash with Ben Fenner's lush, Mellotron mark two string samples supporting the stately 'Slap echo' guitar theme. The tranquil bridge at 2:58 features Doug Sinclair's intricate fretless bass noodling before Mellotron and guitar weigh back in at 4:05. The sustained guitar note at 6:06 seems to go on forever – or to the end of the track at least! Even that most maligned of instruments, the drum machine, doesn't sound out of place here.

'Rise Again' 4:26 (Hackett)

Steve is in a contemplative mood as he reflects on his fascination with the possibilities of reincarnation. This is a song in three parts, with the mellow opening section featuring restrained vocals over an acoustic guitar loop with some wordless harmonies. At 1:45, it shifts up several gears into its uptempo stride. Steve's strained vocals and screaming Gibson Les Paul are driven by Hugo Degenhardt's galloping drum pattern and bass courtesy of Billy Budis. How fortunate Steve was to have such a talented manager. The finale at 3:30 features some intriguing electronic, channel-crossing effects that are best heard through headphones.

'Jane Austen's Door' 6:13 (Hackett)

Like 'Every Day' that opened the *Spectral Mornings* album, this song includes veiled references to Steve's relationship with his first girlfriend in the 1960s, while the gentle pace and evocative lyrical imagery of the song is complemented by his melancholic vocals. References to Jean Paul Sarte, 'Ruby Tuesday', Sloane Square tube station and the novelist of the title are indicators that literature, music and specific places were an important part of their relationship. Sadly, lines like 'Is there a needle beside your hand' and 'A poisoned chalice or the promised land' document her drug addiction and the repeated 'So long' refrain at 2:22 is almost heartbreaking. The arrangement is suitably sparse with Roger King's low-key synths underpinned by a walking rhythm track. The extended ringing guitar coda beginning at 4:28 featuring a double-tracked Les Paul is surprisingly uplifting and very welcome.

'Darktown Riot' 3:10 (Hackett)

This is an instrumental reprisal of the title song, although you would hardly know it as the theme is buried beneath a succession of disorientating effects. Supported by an incessant staccato rhythm – straight out of Queen's 'We Will Rock You' – Steve's Gold Top Les Paul and King's keys weave engaging instrumental textures amongst the barrage of noises. It's not the album's most memorable track, it has to be said, but it's an interesting experiment in sound. The title reflects that the children of 'Darktown' are retaliating against their abusers.

'In Memoriam' 7:59 (Hackett)

This is a very spiritual and personal song with a message; that even when stripped of everything we hold dear, the spirit lives on. In the lyrics, Steve is again looking back to his past where, despite mistakes being made, he has no regrets. Musically, he is also drawing on the past and paying homage to his influences, in this case, King Crimson's 'Epitaph'. The 1969 *In the Court of the Crimson King* album clearly left a lasting impression on the nineteen-year-old Hackett.

A stately Mellotron-style theme underscores the moody lead vocal, buoyed by haunting multi-tracked harmonies. The mellow guitar refrain evokes Robert Fripp at his most melodic while ex-Crimson man John Wetton provides the rumbling bass. Steve's treated guitar is responsible for the colourful, bugle-like fills, which sound remarkably like a synth. Along with the title song, 'In Memoriam' is one of the few tracks to have any longevity as a stage number, where it was regularly performed until 2002.

Related Tracks

The 2013 UK and European reissue of *Darktown* includes three bonus tracks, 'Flame', 'Comin' Home to the Blues' and 'Fast Flower', adding fifteen minutes to the playing time. All three had been previously available to fans in Japan, although on separate albums.

'The Well At The World's End' 3:52 (Hackett)

This instrumental – along with 'Comin' Home To The Blues' – was a bonus track on the original 1999 Japanese edition of *Darktown*. The title comes from the fantasy novel by William Morris, first published in 1896 which strongly influenced both C. S. Lewis and J. R. R. Tolkien. Despite the title, this is actually a cover of Peter Green's twelve-bar instrumental 'The Supernatural' that was first released by John Mayall and The Bluesbreakers in 1967. Like Green, Steve's dazzling soloing makes effective use of sustain and is backed by a slow, samba rhythm.

'Comin' Home To The Blues' 6:12 (Hackett)

This track was recorded circa 1996-1998 during the *Darktown* sessions. Following the *Blues with a Feeling* album, Steve was eager to revisit the genre. The result is a rousing tribute to Sonny Boy Williamson and all the other – now-departed – blues heroes from his past. The lyrics were written with a friend from his school days, Gordon 'Jock' Greenway who introduced Steve to the playing of Eric Clapton when he was a member of John Mayall's Bluesbreakers. On this particular track, however, it's Steve's harmonica playing that dominates.

'Flame' 4:21 (Hackett)

Also recorded sometime between 1996 and 1998, this was previously released on the Japanese edition of *To Watch the Storms* in 2003. It's a captivating, slow-paced ballad in which the song's protagonist is longing to be reunited with a lost love. Steve's singing sounds refreshingly natural and untreated, unlike many of his vocal recordings. His acoustic guitar solo at 1:30 is a delight as are Jerry Pearl's restrained orchestral keys. Billy Budis provides bass.

'Fast Flower' 4:32 (Hackett)

Recorded in 2007, this was originally released on the 2009 Japanese edition of *Out of the Tunnel's Mouth* – see later chapter.

Feedback 86 (2000)

Personnel:
Steve Hackett: guitar, vocals, harmonica
Nick Magnus: keyboards, virtual drums, piano
Chris Thompson: vocals
Brian May: guitar on 'Cassandra', 'Slot Machine', vocals on 'Slot Machine'
Pete Trewavas: bass on 'Cassandra'
Ian Mosley: drums on 'Cassandra'
Bonnie Tyler: vocals on 'Prizefighters'
Terry Pack: bass on 'Prizefighters'
The Phil Henderson Orchestra on 'Prizefighters'
Produced by Steve Hackett, except 'Slot Machine' produced by Steve Hackett and Brian May
Recording date: 1986 – 1987
Release date: 9 October 2000
Record label: UK: Camino Records, USA: Inside Out Music
Highest chart places: UK: Did not chart, USA: Did not chart
Running time: 37:20

Surprisingly, Steve marked the new millennium by taking a regressive, fourteen years step backwards. The material for *Feedback 86* was recorded in 1986 and '87 for the potential follow-up to the *Till We Have Faces* album. Some songs had also been written for the ill-fated second GTR album before Steve decided to jump ship. After working with Steve Howe, he was keen to develop a writing and recording partnership with another well-known guitarist, Brian May and that same year of 1986, May and Queen broke box office records around the world with their *Magic Tour*. Despite Steve's success with GTR and May's involvement, he wasn't able to attract record company interest and the album was put on ice, with legal wrangles further delaying its release.

Unfortunately, the passing of time between recording and release had not treated the songs too kindly, but it's not for want of a solid line-up of collaborators. The Marillion rhythm section features on the lead song while May adds his distinctive guitar sound to two tracks. Chris Thompson of Manfred Mann's Earth Band is the lead vocalist on the majority of the songs, joined by Bonnie Tyler on the GTR leftover 'Prizefighters'. It was also the last album to feature keyboardist Nick Magnus in a major role, having worked with Steve since the *Please Don't Touch!* tour in 1978.

Because of its perceived commercial and dated musical tendencies, the general reception to *Feedback 86* was lukewarm at best. It was however, an opportunity for fans to hear a collection of 'lost' songs that would have otherwise remained gathering dust on the shelf. The songs are very much of their time and the album was never intended as a successor to *Darktown* - it would be more than two and a half years before that arrived.

As it's a short album by CD standards, the 'enhanced' CD features bonus material including video extracts from *The Tokyo Tapes* and MP3 files. The cover features Steve's name in bold capitals with the album title barely legible. The artwork was painted in 1987 and is titled 'Blood on the Rooftops', in a throwback to the ornate style of the 1970s album sleeves. It depicts a middle-aged couple watching TV while taking tea at the bottom of a lake.

'Cassandra' 4:07 (Steve Hackett)

The opening song is firmly grounded in mid-1980s arena rock, sounding like an outtake from the GTR album. The always excellent Chris Thompson does his best to inject some emotion into the one-word choral hook, but the lacklustre melody lets him down. It was slated for possible release as a single but unsurprisingly failed to materialise in that format. Steve's ringing guitar hook is the song's best feature while Pete Trewavas' plodding bass riff and Ian Mosley's metronome drumming lack their customary zeal. The instrumental coda beginning at the two and a half minute mark gives Steve and Brian May the opportunity to rock out with some exhilarating sparring.

'Prizefighters' 5:13 (Hackett, Steve Howe)

This was performed by GTR on their 1986 tour and if the planned second album with Hackett had materialised, this would certainly have been included. It's a simple story of an ageing boxer who is past his best. Max Bacon sang it live and here Bonnie Tyler and Chris Thompson – exchanging the verses and combining for the chorus – turn it into a power ballad. It's certainly a memorably tuneful offering and back in 1986, it would have made a fine single. The instrumental bridge at 2:50 is superb with Steve's stately guitar supported by Terry Pack's full-bodied bass lines. Nick Magnus is responsible for the organ and keyboard orchestrations with compelling pizzicato strings, but it's a pity that the Phil Henderson Orchestra isn't more prominent in the mix.

'Slot Machine' 4:23 (Hackett, Brian May)

Steve and Brian wrote several songs together, but this was the only one they recorded. It's a light-hearted tale about the pitfalls of compulsive gambling. Following the spoken verse intro, we are again transported back to the mid-1980s and it's not a particularly rewarding journey. With its incessant choral hook, big harmonies and gated drum sound, the song is all bluster and no substance, despite Chris Thompson's spirited singing. It's hard to imagine that the combined talents of Hackett and May could not come up with something more inspired than this. Perhaps they cancelled each other out. Again, it's their inventive guitar exchanges and soloing that stand out rather than the lightweight song.

'Stadiums of the Damned' 4:42 (Hackett)

Recorded in 1987, this was influenced by Fyodor Dostoevsky's nineteenth-century novel *Crime and Punishment*. In the book, the central character

Raskolnikov is forgiven by the niece of the victim he's murdered. Steve updates the story to a present-day setting and relates it to a football hooligan who similarly finds redemption thanks to the love of a good woman.

Another atmospheric intro gives way to bombastic keys before Steve's reverb-drenched vocals enter at 1:14 on a bouncing synth rhythm. Incorporating sampled sounds from the football terraces, the mood is a tad too jaunty given the subject, but the chorus is catchy and the quirky instrumental diversions that bring to mind psychedelic era Beatles are engaging. Like the closing song 'The Gulf', this had previously been released as a bonus track on the 1994 CD reissue of the *Till We Have Faces* album.

'Don't Fall' 4:25 (Hackett)

This is a cautionary tale in which the protagonist is warning that he is not the right person with whom to fall in love. It features the stripped-back trio of Hackett, Magnus and Thompson but is none the worse for that. It's a punchy affair with a decent hook driven by Magnus' weighty rhythm track. Steve exchanges harmonica in the first half of the song for guitar in the second, while Thompson's vocal remains confident and assured throughout. A version of 'Don't Fall', featuring Brian May has – to date – remained unreleased. 'Don't Fall Away From Me' on *The Unauthorised Biography* compilation from 1992, is said to have derived from this song although they couldn't be more different in themselves.

'Oh How I Love You' 3:58 (Hackett)

This song continues with the same line-up, although this time, the protagonist is embracing love. The title and chorus is a line from the song 'Mad Man Moon' on Genesis' *A Trick of the Tail* album, penned by Tony Banks. This is a tender ballad with Thompson's plaintive singing – double-tracked in the chorus – complemented by a sparse arrangement of piano and nylon guitar. It is the album's most restrained song and a welcome respite.

'Notre Dame des Fleurs' 3:11 (Hackett)

Many of Steve's albums are graced with a classical guitar instrumental and *Feedback 86* is no exception. Like the previous track, it provides a mellow interlude and although beautifully played, it's not one of his most memorable solo offerings.

'The Gulf' 7:21 (Hackett)

Some of the drum tracks recorded for the *Till We Have Faces* album in 1984 were reworked for this closing song, the album's longest by some margin. When Steve wrote the words, he was thinking of the 1979-1981 Iran hostage crisis. Despite their cultural differences, he imagined president Jimmy Carter and Ayatollah Khomeini both praying to God for a resolution. Despite the title, it predates the 1990-1991 middle-east war of the same name and is a reference to the gulf between man and God.

Acoustic guitar and hand drums provide the backing to Steve's lead vocal for this atmospheric song before hitting it's anthemic, 1980s stride with crashing synth stabs and wailing guitar. The cacophonic instrumental bridge portrays the chaos of war before Steve plays out with a bombastic solo over a blues-rock groove. The song's premise and execution are admirable, but somehow it lacks focus. A shorter, 6:30 version missing part of the intro and coda was a bonus track on the 1994 reissue of the *Till We Have Faces* album.

Related Tracks
The 'enhanced' CD contains MP3 files of twenty tracks culled from previous albums, a video and information on Steve Hackett and Camino Records. As the material from the original sessions had been exhausted, it's not surprising that there were no bonus tracks on subsequent reissues.

To Watch the Storms (2003)

Personnel:
Steve Hackett: vocals, guitar, Optigan, harmonica, koto, rainstick, chimes, cuatro (Qualtro)
Roger King: piano, organ, synthesiser, vocoder, research, programming
Rob Townsend: brass, woodwind, whistles, one-man Serpentine chorus marching band
Terry Gregory: basses, pedals, vocals, thunder
Gary O'Toole: acoustic drums, electric drums, vocals, percussion
John Hackett: flute solo on 'Serpentine Song'
Ian McDonald: saxophone on 'Brand New'
Jeanne Downs: backing vocals
Sarah Wilson: cello
Howard Gott: violin
Produced by Steve Hackett
Engineered by: Roger King, Benedict Fenner, Jerry Peal
Recording date: 2003
Release date: 26 May 2003
Record label: UK: Camino Records, USA: Inside Out Music
Highest chart places: UK: Did not chart, USA: Did not chart
Running time: 58:16

Album number sixteen features the first new material since *Darktown* four years earlier. In the interim, Steve had kept himself busy with touring and writing. In 2001 and 2002 he performed in South America, Europe, North America and the UK and two of the most enduring songs on *To Watch the Storms* – 'Mechanical Bride' and 'Serpentine Song' – were road-tested prior to the album's release.

Roger King, John Hackett and Ian McDonald were once again involved in the recording, along with album newcomers Terry Gregory, Rob Townsend and Gary O'Toole. They would form the nucleus of Steve's touring band for several years to come. Gregory and Townsend are jazz musicians at heart, while O'Toole is also a decent singer, often providing lead vocals on stage until his departure in 2018. The album also marked the true beginning of the Hackett and King writing partnership although they had collaborated on the occasional track on *Genesis Revisited* and *A Midsummer Night's Dream*.

Overall, it's another eclectic brew in terms of inspirations and musical styles. Steve viewed the album as almost cinematic, taking the listener on a musical journey to different periods and places, including resurrecting the Optigan, the vintage keyboard instrument he first used on the *Defector* album.

To Watch the Storms was released in the UK and most other regions as a standard edition and a 'special edition' with bonus tracks. The tracklisting below is the standard edition with the bonus tracks in the 'Related Tracks' section. Typically, a different version was released in Japan. It was generally

93

better received than *Darktown* by both fans and critics and praised for its songcraft and quality of production. Sales, however, indicated that Steve was mostly preaching to the converted. The release was supported by a successful tour of the UK throughout October 2003, bookended by dates in Europe and visits to the USA and Japan. The tour stretched into 2004 including several UK venues in March that had been bypassed the previous year.

Long time collaborator Harry Pearce was responsible for the album design which features Kim Poor's 'Diaphanous' painting technique of powdered glass fused on steel. The blue-tinged cover artwork titled 'See No Evil' depicts part of a face with two blank eyes. The 'special edition' includes a 40-page booklet with the lyrics to each track accompanied by illustrations and Steve's extensive liner notes. The Japanese release features very different cover artwork by Kim entitled 'Muslin Sonata' which dates back to 1992.

'Strutton Ground' 3:05 (Steve Hackett)
This is Steve's musical portrait of a place that no longer exists but remains dear to his heart. It was located on Strutton Ground, a narrow cobbled street off London's Victoria Street and it was here that Steve landed his first full-time job in 1966. The song has a suitably nostalgic feel, enhanced by Optigan and acoustic guitar, painting a vivid evocation of times past with place names that stretch from London to Los Angeles. For Steve, it's an unusually tranquil and unassuming song on which to open an album. Had the new millennium mellowed him?

'Circus of Becoming' 3:49 (Hackett)
The answer to my previous question may well be yes because, to begin with at least, this is another lightweight offering. The title is a metaphor for life with all its ups and downs and again there are several lyrical references to London landmarks. The Optigan is once again in evidence providing the jaunty, 1930s style rhythm for the song part. However, this is a track that mixes different musical traits and at 1:59 and 2:55, it explodes into life with a soaring guitar and church organ bridge. When the *To Watch the Storms* tour resumed in 2004, this song, along with 'Frozen Statues', was added to the setlist.

'The Devil Is an Englishman' 4:28 (Thomas Dolby)
This is a rare example of Steve covering someone else's song – aside from Genesis of course. Thomas Dolby was one of the leading lights on the 1980s synth-pop scene and this originally featured on the *Gothic* film soundtrack from 1987. In this version, Steve attempts to capture the bizarre atmosphere of Ken Russell's movie with a sinister vocal, while bassist Terry Gregory and drummer Gary O'Toole lay down a funky rhythm that acknowledges the song's synth-pop origins. Steve and Roger King conjure up all manner of bizarre – and occasionally grating – electronic effects. This track can be filed in the same macabre song category as 'Vampyre with a Healthy Appetite'.

'Frozen Statues' 2:59 (Hackett, Roger King)

Steve is an avid reader and this song was influenced by a trilogy of books written by Dr. Oliver Sacks on the subject of debilitating illnesses. It's a strange subject to attempt to represent musically, but Steve does just that with a sultry, late-night jazz vibe heavily influenced by Chet Atkins. King's hesitant piano occupies the first one minute and ten seconds before Steve's laidback, crooning vocal enters, alternating with Rob Townsend's moody trumpet fills. It's very tasteful and very unusual for Steve, and there's scarcely a guitar in sight. The sound of a TV with the volume turned down low at the beginning of the song was included to capture the ambience of a hospital ward late at night.

'Mechanical Bride' 6:40 (Hackett)

This piece is again inspired by a book, in this case, Marshall McLuhan's 1951 study of American popular culture *The Mechanical Bride: Folklore of Industrial Man*. In Steve's view, it still holds true today and his interpretation is a political protest song with an anti-war theme. It's his answer to King Crimson's '21st Century Schizoid Man' which was similarly scathing in its indictment of politicians and the war in Vietnam. Steve draws liberally from heavy-rock, jazz-rock and Latin rhythms and anyone familiar with the opening song on *In the Court of the Crimson King* will recognise key elements here. They include the cacophonic wall of sound, the single chord during the verse, the accelerating frantic jam sequence, the aggressive atonal guitar and the stop-start rhythmic sections. The only thing missing is Greg Lake's distorted vocal. Mellotron is present, however, an instrument very much in evidence on the rest of Crimson's seminal 1969 album. Steve regularly performed 'Mechanical Bride' between 2001 and 2004 and occasionally in later years.

'Wind, Sand and Stars' 5:08 (Hackett)

Although this is an instrumental, yet another book is the prime mover here, namely Antoine de Saint Exupéry's 1939 autobiography of the same title. It documents his hazardous exploits as an airmail delivery pilot and Steve captures the spirit of adventure with this atmospheric piece. Opening with ambient chords that simulate a plane in flight, Spanish flavoured classical guitar bursts into life at 0:47. Following a flurry of cascading notes, a haunting theme develops which is picked-up by King's symphonic keys and piano at 3:23. From here on, it's a cinematic feast for the ears with a sumptuous melody that brings to mind the work of film composers like Michael Nyman.

'Brand New' 4:41 (Hackett, King)

In this lyrically simple song, Steve is spiritually and emotionally rejuvenated by the changing seasons. It's the album's most conspicuously commercial offering with a rousing vocal melody and a catchy chorus with big AOR-style harmonies that Steve seems to produce with ease. Instrumentally it also has plenty to praise. Bookended by nylon string solos that open and close the song, Steve lays down some heavy-metal guitar volleys, punctuated by Ian McDonald's saxophone stabs. 'Brand New' was regularly performed on the 2003-2004 *To Watch the Storms tours*. In 2003, a 3:37 single edit of the song was released as a digital download – another first for Steve.

'This World' 5:20 (Hackett, Kim Poor)
This is a song which unashamedly ventures into big ballad territory. It started life as two separate songs which Steve merged taking the verse from one and the chorus from the other. A classical guitar once again opens the song, although this time it's a gentle refrain supported by piano. The infectious chorus is suitably lavish with rich, multi-tracked harmonies backed by King's lush keyboard strings and pipe organ. O'Toole and Gregory's walking rhythm pattern is respectfully restrained but effective nonetheless, as is Steve's searing guitar break at 3:50.

'Rebecca' 4:21 (Hackett)
This song not only acknowledges Daphne du Maurier's 1938 novel *Rebecca*, but also Alfred Hitchcock's 1940 film noir adaptation starring Lawrence Olivier and Joan Fontaine. Musically he conveys both sides of the gothic romance that lies at the heart of the story. Double tracked, counterpoint acoustic guitars provide the intro and the song's rhythmic undercurrent, while Steve's three-part harmonies are to the fore for both the verses and the chorus. Once again, King's opulent keyboard orchestrations aided by violin and cello give the whole thing a cinematic gloss. The frantic guitar interlude at the midway point comes as a jolt, but it's tempered by a shuffle rhythm, elegant synth lines and flute.

'The Silk Road' 5:25 (Hackett, King)
With just four lines of words, this is a mostly instrumental piece that utilises indigenous percussive effects – electric and acoustic – to conjure up a westernised musical interpretation of east Asia. Mournful cello, tabla drums, piano, violin, classical guitar, mellotron, a tribal drum pattern and Townsend's soprano sax soloing are just some of the ingredients in this vibrant concoction. The menacing electric guitar theme at 2:18 is reminiscent of 'Please Don't Touch' from 25 years earlier. Appropriately, the title is taken from the ancient network of trade routes that connected the East and West.

'Come Away' 3:13 (Hackett)
This is a joyously upbeat folk song that conjures up images of lazy hot summers in times gone by. The song's protagonist desires to win the heart of the one he loves and Steve uses the Optigan to recreate a Mazurka folk dance rhythm popular in Eastern European weddings. There is also a lyrical reference to the Fourways Inn which is located in the picturesque village of St.Minver, Cornwall, a place obviously close to Steve's heart. Reverb and sample crowd

sounds are utilised to create the impression of a folk band playing live in the open air. Steve simulated the 'musical saw' solo using a sustained guitar note played with a tremolo arm; an unusual but welcome departure.

'The Moon Under Water' 2:14 (Hackett)

This track is a nylon guitar instrumental that harks back to Steve's classical albums. The mood is sweet and sunny and perfectly matches the ambience of the previous track. He once again adopts his dexterous fingering technique to give the impression of two separate guitars being played in unison. The title comes from a 1946 essay by George Orwell which describes an English pub of the same name.

'Serpentine Song' 6:53 (Hackett)

To close the album, Steve delivers one of his best-ever songs. It's a homage to the famous lake located in London's Hyde Park, renowned for its open-air concerts. The park, which he regularly visited with his father, played a significant part in his early family life. 'Serpentine Song' was performed in 2001 and 2002 prior to the album's release and on the 2003-2004 *To Watch the Storms* tours. A stunning version appears on the 2019 *Genesis Revisited Band & Orchestra: Live at the Royal Festival Hall* album.

It's a beautifully structured song and the joy of it is in the detail. Delicate, ringing guitar notes backed by strings open the track. John Hackett's lyrical flute solo at 2:29 followed by a lovely double-tracked acoustic guitar break are just some of its delights. Rob Townsend is credited as the 'One-man Serpentine Chorus Marching Band' adding a swirling flute motif to lift the chorus, while the delicious harmonies in the key of A were influenced in part by King Crimson's 'I Talk to the Wind'. At 4:56, it plays out with John's flute and Townsend's masterful sax soloing.

Related Tracks

The UK 'Special Edition' includes four additional tracks – 'Pollution B', 'Fire Island', 'Marijuana Assassin of Youth' and 'If You Only Knew'. These are integrated with the thirteen tracks from the standard edition. The Japanese release places the bonus tracks at the end and exchanges 'Marijuana Assassin of Youth' for 'Flame' which also appeared on the 2013 UK reissue of *Darktown* – see the earlier chapter.

'Pollution B' 1:00 (Hackett)

In keeping with the title, this is an ominous sounding diversion complete with eerie guitar and keyboard effects.

'Fire Island' 5:25 (Hackett)

Another of Steve's blues tracks influenced by his early heroes like B.B. King and

Paul Butterfield. In the walking blues style, Steve's moody vocal is matched by his stop-start guitar breaks and King's rhythmic organ fills.

'Marijuana Assassin of Youth' 5:50 (Hackett)

Subtitled 'A Mini Musical', the title comes from a 1937 American anti-drugs exploitation flick *Assassin of Youth*. This tongue-in-cheek concoction features musical excerpts from Bach's 'Italian Concerto' for harpsichord (third movement) – played by King on pipe organ, Neal Hefti's 'Batman Theme' and the vintage instrumentals 'Wipeout' written by Bob Berryhill, Pat Connolly, Jim Fuller, Ron Wilson and 'Tequila' written by Danny Flores. Despite the subject matter, everyone seems to be having fun with O'Toole's versatile drumming standing out.

'If You Only Knew' 2:25 (Hackett)

From the ridiculous to the sublime, you could say, with Steve signing off with a pastoral nylon guitar piece rich in harmonics.

Metamorpheus (2005)

Personnel:
Steve Hackett: guitar, orchestral arrangements
Christine Townsend: principle violin, viola
Lucy Wilkins: violin
Richard Stewart: cello
Sara Wilson: cello
Dick Driver: double bass
John Hackett: flute, piccolo
Colin Clague: trumpet
Richard Kennedy: French horn
Roger King: orchestral arrangements
Jerry Peal: additional orchestral arrangements
Produced by Steve Hackett
Engineered by Roger King, Jerry Peal, Benedict Fenner
Recorded at: MAP Studios, London
Recording date: 2004
Release date: 28 March 2005
Record label: UK: Camino Records
Highest chart places: UK: Did not chart, USA: Did not chart
Running time: 56:56

Metamorpheus is Steve's fourth classical album and is credited to 'Steve Hackett & The Underworld Orchestra'. The 'orchestra' comprises eight classically trained musicians including his brother John and previous Hackett collaborator, Dick Driver. Roger King doesn't play on the album, but along with Steve, he's responsible for the arrangements. Like *A Midsummer Night's Dream*, it's based on classic literature and traces the Greek legend of Orpheus and his journey through the Underworld to find his dead wife Eurydice, with Orpheus' metamorphosis at the end of the story inspiring the album's title. The music is all Steve's and bears no relation to Jacques Offenbach's nineteenth-century opera *Orpheus in the Underworld*. It was mostly written in 2004 although several pieces were adapted from the music Steve provided for the 2001 documentary *Outwitting Hitler*.

Like the previous classical albums, the all-instrumental *Metamorpheus* appealed mostly to Steve's core fanbase while critics appreciated its many qualities and his expert guitar playing in particular. To support the release, in March 2005 Steve, Roger and John embarked on the *Acoustic Trio Tour* which took in the UK, Europe, Canada, the USA, Mexico and Japan. In addition to a medley from the album, the setlist included many of Steve's most popular pieces, from his solo repertoire and Genesis and GTR's 'Imagining' was an unlikely inclusion in the set. A recording of the full show at London's Queen Elizabeth Hall on 3 April 2005 was released as the 2 CD *Live Archive 05*.

That same year, the classic Genesis line-up of Steve, Peter Gabriel, Tony Banks, Phil Collins and Mike Rutherford met to discuss a possible reunion tour. *The Lamb Lies Down on Broadway* was proposed, but talks quickly broke down when Gabriel was reluctant to commit.

Harry Pearce was once again responsible for the CD booklet and slipcase design. The cover painting is an expanded view of the same painting used to illustrate the track 'Rebecca' in the booklet for the previous *To Watch the Storms* album. Liner notes are also provided to set the scene for each of the fifteen tracks, although the evocative titles paint their own pictures.

'The Pool of Memory and the Pool of Forgetfulness' 2:15
(Steve Hackett)
To prepare for his earthly journey, Orpheus gazes into the Pool of Memory before drinking from the Pool of Forgetfulness. Three hammered notes from a bell introduce this track and the album. Steve sets the scene with plaintive guitar textures joined by rich orchestral embellishments that belies the modest number of musicians involved.

'To Earth Like Rain' 1:33 (Hackett)
Orpheus is born in Thrace. He's the son of the god Apollo, his spiritual father and Calliope, his earthly mother. The sprightly guitar theme almost dances from the speakers supported by discrete string washes to celebrate the birth of the story's central character.

'Song to Nature' 3:02 (Hackett)
Orpheus' music – played on a lyre given to him by Apollo – has the power to connect with nature and wildlife. Although the story is based on myth, Orpheus' gift, through his music, clearly struck a chord with Steve. A beautifully haunting piece, it has a stately melody with deep, full-bodied guitar chords and a suitably poignant string backing.

'One Real Flower' 3:12 (Hackett)
Orpheus meets Eurydice, the woman of his dreams. His happiness is emphasised by another joyful nylon guitar melody similar to 'To Earth Like Rain'. The orchestra sits this one out.

'The Dancing Ground' 3:02 (Hackett)
Despite her blissful relationship with Orpheus, Eurydice has a vision of pending disaster. The orchestra is back and suitably refreshed, delivering a romantic waltz that could have been lifted from the late nineteenth century and the pen of Richard Straus. Mirroring Eurydice's concerns, the piece takes a more menacing turn in its closing part with sharp string stabs. This time is Steve's turn to take a back seat.

'That Vast Life' 12:27 (Hackett)

The couple look forward to a lifetime of happiness. The album's longest track by some distance, it boasts an opulent melody that brings to mind the rich, symphonic style of Antonín Dvořák with a touch of Aaron Copland. There is nothing overtly flash about Steve's playing here, It's tastefully understated with sympathetic support from the orchestra, gracefully ebbing and flowing to underline the haunting theme. I love the way it almost comes to a stop at the five-minute mark before beginning anew. This album is sometimes referred to as 'chamber music', but that label would be doing tracks like this a disservice. It's one of Steve's most moving pieces – on a classical or rock album.

'Eurydice Taken' 1:48 (Hackett)

On her wedding night, Eurydice is chased into the woods by the god Aristaeus, where she is bitten by a snake, dying instantly. Orpheus is heartbroken. Eurydice's plight is dramatised by a flurry of cascading glissando with Steve's agile fingers flying rapidly over the frets.

'Charon's Call' 3:15 (Hackett)

Orpheus answers the call of the Ferryman and descends to the Isle of the Dead to find Eurydice. It opens with a sad and lonely violin phrase before guitar ripples into view, followed by the full might of the orchestra. Although tinged with sadness, it's a heartwarming arrangement.

'Cerberus at Peace' 2:06 (Hackett)

The three-headed dog that guards the entrance to the Underworld is lulled into a deep sleep by Orpheus playing the lyre. In contrast to the previous track, this brings a note of levity to proceedings with fanfare-like brass and strings in a playful mood - to begin with at least. The second part captures the menacing presence of the sleeping beast.

'Under the World – Orpheus Looks Back' 5:16 (Hackett)

Orpheus meets the God of the Underworld, Hades and his wife, Persephone. Hades tells him that Eurydice can follow him out of the Underworld, but he must not look at her until she reaches the light. When Orpheus reaches the sunlight, he looks back to ensure Eurydice is still behind him but still in darkness, she is whisked back to the Underworld, trapped forever. Shimmering strings create a suitably chilling depiction of this netherworld, underpinned by an ascending marching bolero rhythm. The tempo increases around the three-minute mark as the couple hurry to the surface. There is a note of triumph before a flurry of dissonant strings sends Eurydice plunging back. This is another stunning arrangement, with a tip of the hat to Gustav Holst's 'Mars, the Bringer of War'.

'The Broken Lyre' 3:17 (Hackett)

Unable to forget Eurydice, Orpheus mourns her passing and his musical powers begin to desert him. Steve's high notes create a passable impression of the lyre in this melancholic but tuneful piece. He is joined by the orchestra for a stirring and bittersweet flute-led melody that perfectly conveys Orpheus' heartbreak and loneliness.

'Severance' 3:05 (Hackett)

The frenzied Maenads – the female followers of Dionysus – descend upon Orpheus and tear him apart. They throw his head and lyre into the river Hebrus. Strident, staccato strings convey the sinister intent of the Maenads before they fall upon the hapless Orpheus in an orchestral frenzy. Given the menacing tone, this was clearly adapted from the *Outwitting Hitler* documentary and also has echoes of the 'The Golden Age of Steam' on *Darktown*.

'Elegy' 3:18 (Hackett)

In their remorse, the Maenads transform into Apollo's Muses, collect Orpheus' body parts and bury them at the foot of Mount Olympus. Echoing the title, pastoral flute ushers in the full orchestra with a deep, resonant string arrangement, which, despite the solemn occasion, rises to grandiose heights. This is another magnificent arrangement, matched by the emotive melody.

'Return to the Realm of Eternal Renewal' 2:56 (Hackett)

Orpheus' head and lyre are washed from the river into the sea and onto the shores of the Island of Lesbos. The head becomes a monument and Orpheus' spirit is reunited with Eurydice. Steve has mostly let the orchestra have their head on the last few tracks but this solo outing belongs to him. His cascading arpeggios convey an air of hope, indicating that this story may have a happy ending after all.

'Lyra' 6:36 (Hackett)

At Apollo's command, the lyre is placed amongst the heavens and is transformed into the Lyra constellation. A kind of overture in reverse, the album's pièce de résistance reprises some of the memorable themes in a sweeping symphony for guitar and orchestra. Appropriately, the orchestra subsides at the halfway mark giving Steve the breathing space to play out with a sensitive nylon guitar lament. This is a stunning conclusion to a beautiful – and vastly underrated – album.

Related Tracks

None. A completely self-contained work, unsurprisingly there were no 'special editions', regional variations or bonus tracks on later releases.

Wild Orchids (2006)

Personnel:
Steve Hackett: guitars, electric sitar, harmonica, psaltery, Optigan, voices
Roger King: keyboards, programming, rhythm guitar
John Hackett: principal flute on 'To A Close', 'She Moves in Memories', 'Cedars of Lebanon', riff guitar on 'Ego & Id'
Rob Townsend: saxes, principal flute on 'Linda', alto flute on 'She Moves in Memories', tin whistle, bass clarinet
Gary O'Toole: drums, harmony voices
Nick Magnus: keyboards on 'Ego & Id'
Benedict Fenner: programming on 'Man in the Long Black Coat'
Jerry Peal: backwards voice intro/outro on 'A Dark Night in Toytown'
The Underworld Orchestra:
Christine Townsend: principal violin, viola
Richard Stewart: cello
Dick Driver: double bass
Colin Clague: trumpet
Chris Redgate: oboe, cor anglais
Produced by: Steve Hackett
Engineered by: Roger King, Benedict Fenner, Jerry Peal
Recording date: 2006
Release date: 11 September 2006
Record label: UK: Camino Records, USA: Inside Out Music
Highest chart places: UK: Did not chart, USA: Did not chart
Running time: 57:25

For Steve's eighteenth studio album, The Underworld Orchestra was retained from *Metamorpheus,* albeit with a few personnel changes. Rob Townsend and Gary O'Toole had by now settled in as a regular part of the lineup, but this was the last album, to date, to feature keyboardist, Nick Magnus. He plays on just the one track having worked with Steve since the *Please Don't Touch!* tour in 1978. In addition to the Optigan keyboard making another reappearance, Steve adds the psaltery – a Greek zither – to his growing list of instrumental accomplishments. The CD booklet credits Steve for playing Fernandes electric and K. Yairi acoustic guitars. Although there is no information regarding the recording location, it was probably the now-regular Map Studios in London.

Like *To Watch the Storms, Wild Orchids* was released as a standard edition CD and a 'special edition' with four additional tracks. These are integrated with the other tracks rather than being added at the end, resulting in a different track sequencing for the special edition. The tracklisting on the Japanese edition is different again. For the sake of consistency, the tracklisting below is the UK standard edition with the additional tracks discussed in the 'Related Tracks' section at the end.

Even without the extra tracks, *Wild Orchids* is an eclectic mix that generally went down well with fans and critics alike. It's one of Steve's musical travelogue-style albums that would become more regular in the following years, culminating with *Under a Mediterranean Sky* in 2021. I reviewed the standard edition for the DPRP in 2006 and rated it seven and a half out of ten. The 'special edition' is undoubtedly a more rewarding listen, however.

The CD booklet and slipcase features a single black and white painting of a naked female figure. The booklet design by Harry Pearce, like all of Steve's recent albums, is minimalist and contemporary.

'A Dark Night in Toytown' 3:42 (Steve Hackett, Roger King, Christoph Willibald Glück)

The opening song was first played on the 2004 UK and European *To Watch the Storms – Encore Tour*. A version appeared on the live DVD *Once Above A Time* under the title 'If You Can't Find Heaven' – a line from the song – released the same year. A guarded warning against the allure of drugs, it's one of Steve's most darkly atmospheric songs with lyrical references to a spooky fairground that includes amongst its attractions 'a ghost train to hell'. Eighteenth-century baroque composer Glück gets a writing credit who, similar to Steve, wrote an opera based on the saga of 'Orpheus and Eurydice'.

When I first heard this song back in 2006, it came as a surprise and I felt that I could have very easily tuned into mainstream pop radio by mistake. It certainly has a catchy, ear-friendly melody with urgent staccato strings and a speeding train-like rhythm. The familiar ticking sounds in the bridge section are a striking reminder of 'Clocks' on *Spectral Mornings*. Steve's preoccupation with rail travel explored in 'The Golden Age Of Steam' on *Darktown* continues here; 'A Dark Night In Toytown', along with 'Down Street' and 'A Girl Called Linda' all contain lyrical references to trains and railways. To underline this point, the special edition includes the bonus track 'Transylvanian Express'.

'Waters of the Wild' 5:35 (Hackett, King)

The lyrics to this song are adapted from the 1889 poem *The Stolen Child* by W.B. Yeats. In an album full of diverse ethnic and cultural musical references, Steve and his band take a musical journey to India by way of Morocco. They must have encountered the Beatles en route because the vibrant and psychedelic, Indian raga style is very 1967. Steve shines on electric sitar with Roger King and Rob Townsend creating authentic sounds from keyboards and soprano sax respectively. Gary O'Toole's weighted drum shuffle adds presence, leaving your author with a burning desire for a Chicken Vindaloo!

'Set Your Compass' 3:38 (Steve Hackett, John Hackett)

This is probably the best of several slow songs on the album, although it does sound a little too close to Simon and Garfunkel's 'Scarborough Fair' for comfort. The intricate, counterpoint harmonies emphasise the connection and the chiming acoustic guitar – played on a Zemaitis twelve-string – harks back to the *Voyage of the Acolyte* album and Steve's work with Genesis. Rob Townsend's bass clarinet, beginning at 3:00, adds a Celtic-flavoured coda, sounding almost like the uilleann pipes. In keeping with the music, the lyrics have a dream-like quality, celebrating the freedom of sailing the ocean's waves.

'Down Street' 7:34 (Hackett, King)

Another dark song, this is the album's longest track, thanks to a lengthy instrumental second half. It's an eerie tale of subterranean London with its abandoned stations and underground rivers that date back Victorian times. The first half finds Steve's processed voice adopting the same deep, slowed-down narrated style of 'Darktown' and 'The Devil Is An Englishman'. He creates an effectively sinister atmosphere, although the novelty value of this sub-gothic style was beginning to wear a little thin by this point.

'Down Street' does have its many compensations, however, including an infectious brass riff, unusual percussive effects and Steve's blistering blues-harp solo. Led by searing guitar and heavy drums, the instrumental sequence is a ragbag of styles. A trad-jazz band sequence really swings and the Optigan is used to create a fairground Wurlitzer organ sound. The dramatic, orchestral ending could almost have been lifted from Nino Rota's *The Godfather* film soundtrack.

'A Girl Called Linda' 4:44 (Hackett)

Steve compares this song to a Sunday brunch in the park. With its playful reference to childhood memories, Linda is clearly an imagined friend from the protagonist's deep past. Steve almost seems to sleepwalk his way through this song with its simple 4/4 piano refrain and sparse arrangement. It's enlivened by the instrumental bridge at 1:45 and 3:12 which has an early King Crimson light-jazz groove. Rob Townsend's lyrical flute and Steve's agile acoustic guitar are backed by Dick Driver's moody double bass.

'To A Close' 4:49 (Hackett)

This is an elegant song that's typical of Steve, with layered vocals, acoustic guitar, flute and strings. Lyrically, it's one of his most mature songs, telling the tragic story of a debutante's rise and fall from fame. There's even a line in French. It's a beautifully constructed song and the memorable, ringing guitar motif makes up for the slight melody and absence of a hook in the chorus. I particularly like John Hackett's gorgeous flute, King's celestial organ and the hymn-like vocal bridge at 2:16. The symphonic finale at 4:11 with its romantic, sweeping strings is magnificent.

'Ego and Id' 4:08 (John Hackett, Nick Clabburn)

This is a rare cover (in a sequence of two) although Steve did play guitars on the original version which appeared on John's debut rock album *Checking Out* of *London* in 2005. In stark contrast with the previous track, this is the heaviest song on the album with a monumental, John Bonham style drum pattern from O'Toole and snarling, metallic guitar from Steve. Compared with the original, Steve's husky vocal is deep and low and his showboating guitar soloing makes good use of fretboard tapping and wah-wah. His keyboard partner of old, Nick Magnus adds some deft organ flourishes that might have been a tad higher in the mix.

'Man in the Long Black Coat' 5:07 (Bob Dylan)

At one time, a Dylan cover from Steve would have seemed unlikely, but in the wake of the release of Steve Howe's *Portraits of Bob Dylan* album seven years earlier, it's not so surprising. The song is from Bob Dylan's 1989 album *Oh Mercy* and memorably contains the line 'There's smoke on the water'. Steve takes this dark American folk tale by the scruff of the neck and makes it his own. An atmospheric intro of nocturnal sounds, harmonica, dobro and mandolin style acoustic guitars give way to volleys of muscular electric guitar that brings an air of tension. Steve's vocals are at their most effective, sounding uncannily like Mark Knopfler at times. An unlikely 4:27 single edit of this song was released for promotional purposes in 2006.

'Wolfwork' 4:49 (Hackett)

It's a dog eat dog world, something that Steve effectively portrays in this scathing parody of modern life, which is another song that has its obvious Beatles influences. Following a deceptive – and overtly lush – symphonic introduction, stark Electric Light Orchestra style string stabs and phased vocals finds Steve taking a rare excursion into 'I Am the Walrus' territory. The powerful gated drum pattern, macabre orchestral interludes and soaring guitar flights all add to a compelling listening experience. Steve's infamous hammering technique goes into overdrive for the frantic guitar solo at 3:08.

'Why' 0:47 (Hackett)

A life portrayed in just four lines of verse, this is another musical pastiche and a throwback to the big band sound of the 1940s. Steve is responsible for the parodic crooning while the Optigan provides the nostalgic musical accompaniment. It's cleverly done, but ultimately a touch dispensable.

'She Moves in Memories' 5:00 (Hackett)

One of only two instrumentals on the standard edition of the album, this is an orchestral arrangement of the backing track for 'To a Close', which Steve felt deserved to be heard in its own right. Minus the vocals, it reveals itself to be a romantic piece in the classical baroque style. The sumptuous arrangement showcases the Underworld Orchestra at their best with the seven musicians managing to sound like 50. Given the full orchestral treatment, this would have sat comfortably on the soundtrack to a filmed costume drama. A touch of nylon guitar from Steve would have been even better!

'The Fundamentals of Brainwashing' 3:01 (Hackett)
As the title alludes, this is a song dedicated to all those that are blinded by their own misguided convictions. It's a relatively short and reflective piano-driven offering that put me in mind of 'In Memoriam' on *Darktown*. Steve adds delicate guitar colourings that hover unobtrusively around the fringes, allowing the lead guitar line and layered vocals to soar skywards during the chorus. This is one of those understated songs that deserves repeated plays to be fully appreciated, not least to pick up the meaning of the clever lyrics.

'Howl' 4:31 (Hackett)
The title of this closing instrumental was inspired by the similarly-named 1956 protest poem by American writer Allen Ginsberg. It could almost be a musical accompaniment to Ginsberg's cry against capitalism, exploitation and repression with discordant guitar almost literally screaming in anguish underpinned by a relentless drum pattern. King's cool jazz piano provides an effective counterpoint with the right hand playing the dexterous lead runs while the left handles the chords. Although supremely performed, this is not the most inspired or rewarding track to close an album. For me, 'She Moves in Memories' would have been a far more satisfying option.

Related Tracks
In addition to a CD slipcase and extended booklet, the 'special edition' has four extra tracks – 'Transylvanian Express', 'Blue Child', 'Cedars of Lebanon' and 'Until the Last Butterfly'. The Japanese edition also contains Transylvanian Express' and 'Cedars of Lebanon', plus two different tracks, 'Eruption' and 'Reconditioned Nightmare'.

'Transylvanian Express' 3:44 (Hackett, King, Glück)
On both the special edition and Japanese release, this instrumental opened the album with 'A Dark Night in Toytown' placed towards the end of the disc. It's actually an instrumental variation of the same song with an extended intro, simulating the sound of a slowly accelerating train. Arrangement wise, it's also a more dissonant affair with less emphasis on the melody with the weird – and occasionally wonderful – electronic effects more prominent. The driving string arrangement common to both tracks always reminds me of the 1967 classic 'The Days of Pearly Spencer'.

'Blue Child' 4:25 (Hackett)
The title is another giveaway. This is a slow, mainstream rock instrumental where the stately guitar soloing has a slight blues inflection, underpinned by a

wash of Mellotron-like strings. It has an air of Dutch band Focus about it which is ironic considering the bonus track on the Japanese edition – see below.

'Cedars of Lebanon' 4:02 (Hackett)

Unsurprisingly given the title, this is a song with a distinct Middle Eastern flavour. The title is a biblical reference and Steve's unsettling vocal longs for the past glories of this once great nation. The song section that occupies the first half is driven by a relentless rhythm track while the instrumental second half features superbly evocative orchestrations. I suspect that when it was recorded, this was a strong contender for the standard edition.

'Until the Last Butterfly' 2:29 (Hackett)

Harry Pearce, the man responsible for the album artwork, also provided the title for this nylon guitar instrumental. Steve's playing here is fast but no less intricate for that. One can almost picture the winged insect of the title flitting in and out of the hedgerows.

'Eruption' 3:38 (Thijs van Leer, Tom Barlage)

An instrumental cover lifted from the 'Eruption' suite that takes up side two of Focus' 1971 album *Moving Waves*. It's actually the 'Tommy' section composed by Tom Barlage, sax and flute player with fellow Dutch prog-band Solution. A longer version entitled 'Divergence' appeared on Solution's 1972 album of the same name. It's impossible to listen to this and not compare it with Jan Akkerman's stunning playing on the Focus version. Although Steve and Jan have never performed together to my knowledge, both guitarists came to prominence in the early 1970s and they both featured on the 1973 *Two Sides of Peter Banks* album by the ex-Yes guitarist.

'Reconditioned Nightmare' 4:07 (Hackett)

This is an updated version of the instrumental 'Air Conditioned Nightmare' that originally appeared on the 1981 *Cured* album. Steve was inspired to re-record it after playing it on the 2004 *To Watch the Storms – Encore* tour. If the original version was a relentless onslaught, this thunderous update similarly takes no prisoners. The powerful rhythm – similar to ELP's 'Fanfare for the Common Man' – really swings, propelling Steve and Roger King's gothic soundtrack to a horror movie that never was.

Tribute (2008)

Personnel:
Steve Hackett: classical guitar
Produced by Steve Hackett
Engineered by Roger King
Recorded at: Map Studios, London
Recording date: 2007
Release date: 11 February 2008
Record label: UK: Camino Records
Highest chart places: UK: Did not chart, USA: Did not chart
Running time: 50:47

The aptly titled *Tribute* is Steve's fifth classical album. The recording was
perhaps inspired by the success of the *Acoustic Trio* tours that ran on and off
from 2005. Whereas previous recordings in the genre had consisted mostly of
original material, here he tips his nylon guitar to notable composers like Bach
and Rodrigo. He plays completely solo with no instrumental support from
Roger King, John Hackett or The Underworld Orchestra, although King was
responsible for the recording, compiling and mastering of the tracks.

The album was originally intended as a tribute to twentieth-century classical
guitar virtuoso Segovia before the Bach pieces began to take over. Steve was
inspired by Segovia at the age of fifteen when he first heard him on an album
playing the music of Bach. He marvelled at his intricate playing with its varied
textures and colours. Some of the compositions here were first committed
to record in the 1920s and 1930s and King utilised modern technology to
recapture the ambience of those vintage recordings.

Although Steve's playing acknowledges Segovia, he deliberately avoided
copying previous interpretations of the pieces. Perhaps it's the absence of
other instruments that gives the album a certain clarity, but *Tribute* boasts
Steve's most accomplished acoustic playing on record. Although musically
it's a little dryer, lacking the romanticism of *A Midsummer Night's Dream* and
Metamorpheus, he shows a delicate and florid touch that's both appealing
and relaxing and he certainly compares favourably with classical guitar greats
like John Williams and Julian Bream. The recording required a lot of effort
and Steve remains immensely proud of the album. For the guitar buffs out
there, he plays a K. Yairi classical guitar with D'Addario Pro-Arte light tension
nylon strings.

This would be Steve's final album release on Camino Records, which was
eventually dissolved.

The CD booklet design by Pentagram is suitably tasteful with mostly white
text against a black background. The colour photo on the cover is one of
only two in the booklet. It depicts Steve, eyes closed, totally immersed in his
playing. The inner photo of Roger King is accompanied by some liner notes.
The 2015 reissue on Edel Records contains additional liner notes by Steve.

'Gavottes BWV 1012' 3:59 (Johann Sebastian Bach)

This is the first of six pieces by Bach, probably the most famous composer of the baroque period. Although he didn't write specifically for guitar, many of his pieces have been transcribed for the instrument and in the eighteenth century, Bach himself transcribed several of his suites for lute. This particular arrangement is from his 'Cello Suite No. 6 in D Major, BWV 1012'. BWV – Bach-Werke-Verzeichnis – is a numbering system devised to catalogue his works. Steve deliberately chose this as the opening track as it was the very first music he heard played on classical guitar. Segovia had combined two of Bach's pieces which Steve's sprightly rendition emulates to perfection.

'Courante BWV 1009' 3:05 (Bach)

One of Steve's favourite guitar pieces, this was again originally written for cello – 'Cello Suite No. 3 in C Major, BWV 1009' – where it's played at a slower pace. Given the speed and vigour of his fingerwork, Steve's masterclass here is simply breathtaking.

'Jesu Joy BWV 147' 3:26 (Bach)

'Jesu, Joy of Man's Desiring' is one of Bach's best-known tunes. Steve felt compelled to record it for guitar, particularly given its spiritual connection. It had also informed his composition 'The Lunatic, The Lover & The Poet' on the *A Midsummer Night's Dream* album. While the major key section is suitably joyful, Steve felt the minor section was too robust, so he deliberately applied a softer, more delicate touch there.

'The Fountain Suite' 8:19 (Steve Hackett)

Although written by Steve, this is a homage to Andrés Segovia, the Spanish guitar virtuoso active from 1909 up until the 1980s. Prior to recording it, Steve had previously performed this on stage as 'A Tribute to Segovia'. The longest piece on the album, Steve captures the essence of the maestro without slavishly copying his style. It's a hauntingly beautiful piece and the nylon guitar has rarely sounded sweeter.

'The Earle Of Salisbury' 1:30 (William Byrd)

This is a late-period Pavan from Byrd, written originally for the keyboard. It was composed in 1612 in memory of Robert Cecil, the first Earl of Salisbury, who had died the previous year. Steve was inspired to record it after hearing John Redbourn play it on guitar with folk-rockers Pentangle, although Steve's elegant version is more in the style of Segovia.

'La Catedral' 2:53 (Agustín Barrios)

Paraguayan classical guitarist Agustín Pío Barrios composed and first performed 'La Catedral' in 1921. The original piece is longer, but Steve here concentrates on the livelier Allegro section. Steve describes it himself as intense but fluent with his fingers flying over the strings to emulate falling leaves, capturing Barrios' love of nature and the forest.

'El Noy De La Mare' 2:13 (Traditional)

This piece has a poignant melody based on a traditional Catalan song but there's barely a hint of the Spanish style in Steve's restrained performance. Short and sweet it may be, but this is one of the most evocative pieces on the album.

'Cascada' 3:04 (Hackett)

This is another piece credited to Steve, this time a tribute to Spanish composer Joaquín Rodrigo. He was a virtuoso pianist, but his most famous work is probably the best known and loved guitar concerto of all time, *Concierto de Aranjuez*. Steve spent an evening trying to write an appropriate melody and after giving up, it came to him the following day. Whilst kept in check on the previous track, the Spanish influence blossoms on this sunny delight.

'Sapphires' 1:41 (Hackett)

The writing of this piece dates back to the 1960s and was Steve's first successful attempt to create a solo guitar work in the 'early music' style. Described as 'A Tudor Tribute', it has a courtly elegance that perfectly captures the opulence of Henry VIII's court.

'Prelude In D, BWV 998' 1:49 (Bach)

Back to Bach and we find him in a joyful, playful mood. It's a short piece which is just as well because Steve races through it, hardly pausing for breath. Once again, it's his nimble-fingered performance that takes the breath away.

'Prelude In C Min, BWV 999' 1:14 (Bach)

This piece is shorter still, but harmonically it's an elaborate piece. Similar to the previous track, this has a sprightly spring in its step with Steve's impressive note clusters flying from the nylon strings at a rapid rate.

'Chaconne BWV 1004' 12:35 (Bach)

The final movement from 'The Partita in D minor', Bach wrote this piece for solo violin in memory of his first wife who died in 1720. It was later transcribed for piano by several composers including Brahms. For Steve, it works best as a guitar piece and is one of the most difficult to play. With a love of Bach dating back to his teens, this was the first track recorded for the album.

If Steve's playing on the previous tracks had impressed, here it astounds. The flurry of notes in the first half have jazz-like agility of which John Mclaughlin would be proud. Around the halfway mark, it changes from minor to major keys and Steve's playing is more restrained but no less dexterous. If you listen to just one of Steve's classical guitar solos to fully appreciate his mastery of the instrument, this has to be it.

'La Maja de Goya' 4:59 (Enrique Granados)

For the final track, we leave Germany behind and return to the sunnier climes of Spain. Premiered in 1911, this was part of a six-piece piano suite by Granados, inspired by the paintings of Francisco Goya. It was transcribed for guitar by Miguel Llobet and has that distinct Spanish timbre. Steve adopts his 'small orchestra' technique to create different tones, textures and colours to bring the album to a sparkling conclusion.

Related Tracks
'Through the Trees' 3:30 (Hackett)

This is the sole bonus track on the 2015 reissue of *Tribute,* remastered by Roger King. It is Steve's 'Tribute to Nature' and it's not hard to tell why. Inspired by Bach, the piece has a waltz-like elegance at times, capturing the pastoral beauty of the subject. In contrast, Steve also incorporates some of the more rapid flights that distinguished 'Chaconne'.

Out of the Tunnel's Mouth (2009)

Personnel:
Steve Hackett: vocals, guitars
Roger King: keyboards, programming
Nick Beggs: bass guitar, Chapman stick on all tracks except 'Fire on the Moon',
'Tubehead', 'Last Train to Istanbul'
Anthony Phillips: twelve-string guitar on Emerald and Ash', 'Sleepers'
Chris Squire: bass guitar on 'Fire on the Moon', 'Nomads'
Dick Driver: double bass on 'Sleepers'
Christine Townsend: violin, viola on 'Sleepers', 'Ghost in the Glass', 'Last Train to
Istanbul'
Ferenc Kovacs: violin on 'Last Train to Istanbul'
John Hackett: flute on 'Sleepers', 'Last Train to Istanbul'
Amanda Lehmann: backing vocals on 'Emerald and Ash', 'Sleepers', 'Still Waters'
Jo Lehmann and Lauren King: backing vocals on 'Still Waters'
Rob Townsend: soprano sax on 'Emerald and Ash', 'Last Train to Istanbul'
Produced by Steve Hackett and Roger King
Engineered by Roger King
Recorded at The Living Room
Recording date: 2007 – 2009
Release date: 30 October 2009
Record label: UK: Wolfwork Records, USA: Inside Out Music
Highest chart places: UK: 173, USA: Did not chart
Running time: 45:42

Steve's twentieth studio album continued his upward trajectory in terms of
the quality of its material and a return to his prog-rock style. In addition to
Roger King co-writing five out of the eight tracks, Steve's new partner, writer
Joanna Lehmann, is credited on four songs. Jo's sister Amanda would feature
on future albums and from 2009, as part of the touring band on vocals and
guitar. She also designed a new website for Steve – *hackettsongs.com* – which
continues to this day. While there is no concept as such, *Out of the Tunnel's
Mouth* continues Steve's fascination with trains, especially the steam-driven
variety. There are also several songs based on his world travels, which could be
described as musical postcards.

The album was recorded using Steve's home studio set-up and constructed
on computer by Roger King using Apple Logic. It boasts the most prestigious
line-up of guests since *Feedback 86* in 2000. His Genesis predecessor
Anthony Phillips plays on two tracks, as does Chris Squire. The Yes bassist
and Steve developed a close friendship and this led to several future
collaborations. It was the first of several albums to feature ex-Kajagoogoo
bassist Nick Beggs who also toured with Steve. In the absence of a drummer,
King's programming provides the convincing rhythms. It was also Steve's first
release in the UK on his new Wolfwork label. The album was initially available

113

in 2009 through his website and tour merchandising. A two-disc 'Special Edition' was released in Europe in May 2010 and in North America in June.

Between March and September 2009, prior to the album's official release, a handful of dates were played in Italy, Germany, Switzerland and Poland including several festivals. Although 'Fire on the Moon', destined for the new album, was played on that tour, the setlist consisted mostly of Genesis tunes and Steve's popular early material. Following a headlining appearance at the *Summers End Festival* on 9 October 2009, Steve and his 'Electric Band' boarded the so-called *Train On The Road Tour* which ran through mainland Europe and the UK. The album was well represented by 'Fire on the Moon', 'Emerald and Ash', 'Ghost in the Glass', 'Tubehead', 'Sleepers' and 'Still Waters'. The tour continued in 2010, taking in Europe, America, Canada, Japan and London's prestigious *High Voltage* Festival on 25 July. By the time it hit the rest of the UK in the latter part of the year, it was being dubbed the *Around the World in 80 Trains* tour and was Steve's most extensive in several years.

The cover photo by Jo Lehmann is apt, showing Steve, guitar case in hand, on a railway platform shrouded in steam. His name and the album title are in bold graphics. The CD booklet for the 'Special Edition' contains a good selection of photos of Steve and band in action.

'Fire on the Moon' 6:11 (Steve Hackett)

Following a gentle child-like intro to the chimes of a musical box – a recurring sequence throughout the song – the album gets off to a humdinger of a start with this mighty and majestic track. It's the kind of song that Steve does so well, oozing restrained power with his own massed choral chant backed by a powerful bolero rhythm. Chris Squire's dynamic bass lines and Roger King's grandiose keys play their part and the soaring guitar solos at 2:45 and 4:34 are a perfect fit. As well as launching the album, this was one of the opening songs during the 2009 European tour dates. One of Steve's most personal offerings, it's a song about loss and the pain that it brings. It also reflects on the fears that linger from early childhood memories, emphasised by the musical box motif.

'Nomads' 4:31 (Hackett, Jo Lehmann)

This is a homage to Andalucia, flamenco music and the free spirit of the Spanish gipsies. It was written by Steve and Jo following a trip to the Sacromonte caves in Granada, southern Spain. Following superb Spanish guitar picking and a restrained song section with delightful harmonies, at 2:35 it develops into a rousing flamenco dance complete with authentic castanets and handclaps. You can almost smell the olives and fruit trees. As it starts to rock out, Squire's thunderous bass once again makes its presence felt while the raunchy guitar break features two of Steve's infamous Fernandes sustains. Together, they last a combined – and ear-piercing – 30 seconds.

'Emerald and Ash' 8:59 (Hackett, Roger King)

Opening with Rob Townsend's sweet soprano sax and King's keys strings, the first half of this song is in laidback mode. When the album was first released, the tune was naggingly familiar, reminding me of a pop ballad from the 1970s but I couldn't put my finger on it. Eleven years on, I'm still pulling my hair out – or what's left of it – trying to identify the song. There's no mistaking the heavenly acoustic interlude at 4:03, however, featuring the twelve-string chords of Ant Phillips.

At 5:38, the piece introduces a monumental riff that sounds like a cross between Led Zeppelin and *Red* era King Crimson. Electric guitar howls aggressively over the top of a punchy rhythm courtesy of King's virtual drums and Nick Beggs' bass. Lyrically, the song is a warning against being lulled into a false sense of security and that danger may be lurking just around the corner. 'Emerald and Ash' was one of several of the album's songs still being regularly played on the 2011 tour and it occasionally opened the set.

'Tubehead' 3:36 (Hackett, King)

The album's first instrumental, the fast and furious 'Tubehead' has all the energy of a gale-force wind with Steve's manic guitar screaming and wailing for all its worth. It was co-written by King who was responsible for the thundering bass intro and the runaway train rhythm. Heavy metal is rarely as good as this.

'Sleepers' 8:50 (Hackett, King, Lehmann, Nick Clabburn)

This is a song about dreams and nightmares, one of Steve's recurring themes. Another lengthy track, this centrepiece is probably my favourite song on the album and is divided into three distinct sections.

It opens with a beautifully romantic classical guitar and strings arrangement reminiscent of the epic 'Mont St. Michel' that closed Mike Oldfield's 1996 *Voyager* album. For me, this part could have gone on forever, but following Ant's twelve-string bridge, there's a graceful transition at 2:35 into a plaintive song in which Steve's voice is at its most wistful. For the chorus, he is supported by the lovely harmonies of Amanda Lehmann. At 4:51, it finally succumbs – like many of the songs here – to a heavyweight rhythm with backward effects, distorted vocals and equally distorted guitar histrionics. To its credit, through all of this, it still manages to remain tuneful before subsiding for the serene outro.

'Ghost in the Glass' 2:59 (Hackett, King)

In his CD liner notes, Steve describes the album's second instrumental as 'The ghost of the past meets the ghost of the future'. It opens with a tranquil Spanish guitar and sampled birdsong sequence before taking flight with a scorching, feedback laced, electric solo against a backing of strings. It's in the same style, but not quite in the same class as 'Twice Around The Sun' on the *Darktown* album from 10 years earlier, despite Nick Beggs' dazzling fretless bass playing.

'Still Waters' 4:35 (Hackett, Lehmann)

Back to Steve's liner notes, where he describes the penultimate track as 'The pulse of New Orleans – Storyville put to song'. The lyrics contain references to the mystical undertone of this vibrant city including the tradition of Voodoo. The title is almost a contradiction in itself with heavy and bluesy guitar-shredding sitting – a little uncomfortably – alongside the anthemic chorus with its lush female harmonies. The combined voices of Amanda Lehmann, Jo Lehmann and Lauren King are simply superb in this 'Blues meets Gospel' excursion in 6/8 time.

'Last Train to Istanbul' 5:56 (Hackett, King, Lehmann)

The final track is inspired by the Turkish music that Steve heard on his travels in Sarajevo – clearly, the Bosnian's had a penchant for Turkish music. Familiar Hackett themes, including train imagery and his travelogue, world music style are explored in this atmospheric song. It has a Middle Eastern flavour that teases the senses, conjuring up images of Turkish bazaars and mosques. Like so many of the tracks here, it begins slowly before building the atmosphere layer by layer. King lays the foundations with his ethnic-sounding keyboard arrangements, providing a backdrop for the virtuoso soloing. Steve, for his part, provides the sitar-like guitar. The playing of Hungarian violinist Ferenc Kovaks is stunning while Rob Townsend and John Hackett give impressive soprano saxophone and flute performances respectively. It's a satisfying conclusion to a very satisfying album.

Related Tracks

The two-CD 'Special Edition' contains a bonus disc with nearly 33 minutes of additional material. Five out of the six tracks were recorded live in Italy and these include four of Steve's favourite Genesis tunes. In Japan, the main CD featured two additional tracks, 'Fast Flower' and 'Every Day'.

'Blood on the Rooftops' 5:46 (Phil Collins, Hackett)

This is the first of five tracks recorded live in Italy during the March 2009 leg of the European tour. The band featured Roger King (keyboards), Nick Beggs (bass, Chapman stick, vocals), Gary O'Toole (drums, vocals) and Rob Townsend (sax, flute, whistle, percussion). This song is arguably Steve's best songwriting contribution to Genesis and is still performed on nylon guitar.

'A Tower Struck Down' 4:27 (Steve Hackett, John Hackett)

This is a worthy, heavyweight version of this instrumental from Steve's 1975 debut album *Voyage of the Acolyte*. The spiky interplay between the instruments – especially guitar and sax – is spot on.

'Firth of Fifth' 10:10 (Tony Banks, Collins, Peter Gabriel, Hackett, Mike Rutherford)

When Genesis performed this song on the 1973 *Selling England by the Pound* tour, Tony Banks often wrestled with the solo piano intro and he eventually omitted it from the performance. Here, King nails it perfectly, including the seamless transition from piano to organ.

'Fly on a Windshield' 2:19 (Banks, Collins, Gabriel, Hackett, Rutherford)
When this was performed on the 1974-1975 *The Lamb Lies Down on Broadway* tour, Steve experimented with the guitar solo as he also does here. King's eerie Mellotron and Beggs' plodding bassline sound just like the original, however.

'Broadway Melody of 1974' 2:03 (Banks, Collins, Gabriel, Hackett, Rutherford)
Segueing seamlessly from the previous track, O'Toole gives a very credible vocal performance as he does on all this batch of live songs, especially 'Blood on the Rooftops'.

'Every Star in the Night Sky' 8:05 (Hackett, King, Clabburn, Lehmann)
This is a remix of 'Sleepers' with elements of 'Still Waters' from the main album. Both songs are virtually unrecognisable and reminded me of the twelve-inch single remixes that were popular in the early 1980s. Opening with a nylon guitar solo, it goes through a myriad of changes with Steve's phased vocals and King's heavy drum track to the fore. The guitar and keyboard exchanges alone make this well worth seeking out and Steve throws in a manic harmonica solo for good measure. On this track, Steve and Jo, along with Egerhazi Attila, Barabas Tamas, Kovacs Ferenc, Kovacs Zoltan and Banai Szilard are credited with playing the angklung, an Indonesian percussive instrument.

'Fast Flower' 4:31 (Hackett)
This is a leftover track from the album sessions, featuring Chris Squire on bass. The song is about escape and living life in the fast lane. A foot-tapping, mid-tempo blues-rock song, the lead guitar is suitably edgy and Steve's mannered vocal is typical of the genre. His guitar is more inventive with all manner of effects including sustain, note bending, dive bombs and string tapping. 'Fast Flower' was also one of three bonus tracks on the 2013 UK and European reissue of *Darktown*.

'Every Day' 6:57 (Hackett)
This is an excellent live version of the opening song from *Spectral Mornings* recorded at the 1,300 capacity Club Citta in Kawasaki, Japan. The band line-up features King on keyboards, Lee Pomeroy on bass, O'Toole on drums, Amanda Lehmann on guitar, vocals and Townsend on soprano sax, vocals.

Beyond the Shrouded Horizon (2011)

Personnel:
Steve Hackett: guitars, vocals, harmonica
Roger King: keyboards, programming
Nick Beggs: bass, Chapman stick, ukulele on 'Loch Lomond', 'A Place Called Freedom'
Dick Driver: double bass on 'Til These Eyes', 'Between the Sunset and the Coconut
Palms', 'Looking for Fantasy', 'Turn This Island Earth'
John Hackett: flute on 'Two Faces of Cairo', vocals on 'Between the Sunset and the
Coconut Palms'
Amanda Lehmann: vocals on various, guitar on 'Prairie Angel', 'A Place Called Freedom'
Gary O'Toole: drums on various, vocals on 'Loch Lomond', 'A Place Called Freedom'
Simon Phillips: drums on 'Catwalk', 'Turn This Island Earth'
Chris Squire: bass on 'Looking for Fantasy', 'Catwalk', 'Turn This Island Earth'
Richard Stewart: cello & Christine Townsend: violin, viola on 'Til These Eyes',
'Between the Sunset and the Coconut Palms', 'Two Faces of Cairo', 'Looking for
Fantasy'
Rob Townsend: sax, whistle, bass clarinet
Produced by Steve Hackett and Roger King
Recorded, mixed and mastered by: Roger King at Map Studios, London
Recording date: 2010 – 2011
Release date: 26 September 2011
Record label: UK: Wolfwork Records, USA: Inside Out Music
Highest chart places: UK: 133, USA: Did not chart
Running time: 57:52

Despite the protracted 2010 world tour which continued well into the summer
of 2011, Steve found time to marry Jo Lehmann on the 4 June and record
studio album number 21. The couple, along with the inimitable Roger King,
co-wrote all the new material on *Beyond the Shrouded Horizon,* although two
tracks were reworked, previously unreleased songs from the GTR period.

Although there is no concept as such, world travel – like many of Steve's
albums – provides a common thread, evident in tracks like 'Loch Lomond',
'Wanderlust', 'Between the Sunset and the Coconut Palms' and 'Two Faces of
Cairo'. Five of the thirteen tracks – the largest number on any Hackett single disc
– are instrumentals. In the liner notes, Steve describes it as 'A full-throttle ride
from the shores of Loch Lomond to the Rings of Saturn'. With the exception of
the near twelve-minute closing song 'Turn This Island Earth', the album contains
some of Steve's shortest tracks to date, although many buyers were tempted by
the 'Special edition' bonus CD which contained a further nine tracks.

The touring band were once again the nucleus for the recording, with
additional support from Chris Squire and esteemed drummer Simon Phillips,
who is noted for his work with Mike Oldfield and The Who amongst many
others. Gary O'Toole makes a welcome return following the blanket use of
programmed drums on the previous studio album.

The album was very well received by fans and critics alike and hailed as one of Steve's best of the new millenium. The release was closely followed by the so-called *Breaking Waves* tour which included a handful of European and UK dates in October and November 2011 before resuming in earnest in March 2012. Dates followed in Europe with a return to Rome in April which had become a popular port of call for Steve. In the early 1970s, Italy was one of the first nations to take Genesis to their hearts and its people were rewarded with a mammoth free concert in Rome during the *Turn It On Again* tour in 2007.

The blue-tinted cover photo is as evocative as any could be, perfectly conveying the travelogue theme and regular designer Harry Pearce was the man behind the lens.

'Loch Lomond' 6:49 (Steve Hackett, Jo Hackett, Roger King)

Distorted guitar provides the moody intro to both this song and the album, backed by keyboard strings. A gritty rock instrumental sequence follows, powered by a relentless stop-start rhythm from Gary O'Toole and Nick Beggs. There is a change of pace at 1:56 for the pastoral song section where Steve's double-tracked vocals are joined by O'Toole and Amanda Lehmann's sweet harmonies for the chorus. The lyrics paint an atmospheric picture of wintertime by the scenic shores of the famous lake situated in south-west Scotland. At 4:10, a haunting instrumental interlude features the sound of bagpipes courtesy of samples and Rob Townsend's sax – with a touch of manipulation. When the song proper kicks back into gear the choral crescendo at 5:37 is stunning, bringing Yes to mind.

'The Phoenix Flown' 2:08 (S. Hackett, J. Hackett, King)

This is a fairly short instrumental with a memorable, mid-tempo melody. Steve's ringing guitar soloing is some of his most compelling and tuneful since 'Twice Around the Sun' on the *Darktown* album. Sustain is kept mostly controlled and I particularly like the upward glissando at 0:43, perfectly capturing the born-again essence of the mythical bird in the title. On the subsequent *Breaking Waves* tour, 'Loch Lomond' and 'The Phoenix Flown' were the doubleheaders that opened the set.

'Wanderlust' 0:44 (S. Hackett, J. Hackett, King)

This is an even shorter instrumental – a nylon guitar solo, which by now, was almost obligatory on a Steve Hackett album. Strings are plucked in his usual skilful manner and the title aptly describes his free spirit and penchant for travel.

'Til These Eyes' 2:41 (S. Hackett, J. Hackett, King)

This continues the mood of the previous track with acoustic guitar and orchestral strings supporting a romantic ballad. Steve's singing is neither processed nor multi-tracked, giving it a welcome vulnerability that's perfectly in keeping with the tone of the song. It's an ode to the power of love to transform and rejuvenate. Cleary, Steve was inspired by his recent romance and union with Jo.

'Prairie Angel' 2:59 (S. Hackett, J. Hackett, Steve Howe, Jonathan Mover)

This song is a throwback to the GTR period. With Jo's assistance, Steve breathed new life into this instrumental, which opens with a stately guitar and strings theme. It is inspired by Jack Kerouac's 1957 novel *On the Road*, which relates to the author's travels across America. The aggressive, stop-start section that takes over at 1:44 is pure, heavy blues-based rock. With harmonica to the fore, the playing gets increasingly faster, building to a fever pitch. Perhaps unsurprisingly it was played on the 2011 tour alongside 'A Place Called Freedom'.

'A Place Called Freedom' 5:57 (S. Hackett, J. Hackett, King)

Following on from the previous track, this is a love story set in the days when America's native population freely roamed the open plains. Steve was inspired by his own long-distance travels by road across the wide-open spaces and he gives the song a distinct Americana sound, painting a vast canvas with music. The combination of dobro-like acoustic guitar, organ, harmonica, jaws harp and Steve's accented vocal has the unmistakable flavour of American folk. Elsewhere, the song has a suitably panoramic sound with Amanda and O'Toole once again backing Steve for the expansive choral harmonies. The instrumental bridge at 2:52 reprises the stately guitar theme from 'Prairie Angel' and the soaring coda at 4:54 makes full use of the Fernandes sustainer for those extra long notes.

'Between the Sunset and the Coconut Palms' 3:18 (S. Hackett, J. Hackett, King)

According to Steve's liner notes, the title was inspired by a Peter Sellers sketch although I can find no reference to it on the internet. The evocative lyrics contemplate a nighttime boat ride into the freedom of open waters. It's a sparsely arranged song with Steve's reflective, multi-tracked vocals backed by strummed acoustic guitar chords. Reverb is added to create a haunting echo for the chorus which, curiously, reminds me of The Beach Boys' 'Don't Worry Baby'. At 2:16, Christine Townsend's evocative violin cadenza sets the scene for a lush orchestral arrangement of the song section to bring the track to a majestic close.

'Waking to Life' 4:50 (S. Hackett, J. Hackett, King)

Following loosely in the footsteps of 'The Silk Road' and 'Waters of the Wild', this is another of Steve's lively Asian, raga style tunes that he does so brilliantly. In keeping with the title, it has an air of exuberant authenticity; from Amanda's superb lead vocal – something she should do more often – to wailing guitar, violin, sax, rhythmic keys and sitar-like guitar. A wonderfully exotic concoction, it was deservedly played on the 2011-2012 tour, allowing Amanda to take centre stage. Like 'Til These Eyes', it's a tribute to love's dream.

'Two Faces of Cairo' 5:13 (S. Hackett, J. Hackett, King)

Like 'Valley of the Kings' on the *Genesis Revisited* album, the inspiration for this instrumental came from a trip to Egypt and specifically the Great Sphinx of Giza located on the outskirts of Cairo. It's a celebration of Egypt's past glories in stark contrast with its less illustrious present. Like 'Waking to Life', this piece has a beautiful attention to detail, creating an atmospheric evocation of the location and period. Following the ambient intro, O'Toole's primal, but articulate drum pattern thunders into life, bringing with it expressively Middle Eastern-tinged orchestrations, while Steve's high pitched guitar convincingly impersonates the shrill sound of an Egyptian flute. It's all great stuff and it has a pretty decent tune to boot.

'Looking for Fantasy' 4:33 (S. Hackett, J. Hackett, King)

This is one of Steve's most evocative songs, relating the story of an ageing spinster attempting to recapture her youth of the 1960s. It's full of lyrical references to the decade including the King's Road, the Kennedys and *Women in Love* – the Ken Russell film, rather than the book. Musically, however, the song feels like it is derived from an earlier setting, sounding like something from the 1940s. Only the choral hook with Steve's full-bodied, three-part harmonies places it in contemporary times. Elsewhere, the timbre of the subdued orchestral intro, acoustic guitar bridge and the mournful violin backing Steve's plaintive verses, have a distinct period feel. It's a song in Steve's canon that's easily overlooked but very rewarding nonetheless.

'Summer's Breath' 1:12 (S. Hackett, J. Hackett, King)

The title says it all. This is a short, but expressive nylon guitar solo where the swirling note clusters resonate like the morning sun.

'Catwalk' 5:44 (S. Hackett, J. Hackett, King)

This is one of Steve's blues-based excursions and it tells of a woman's rise from humble beginnings to a much-admired fashion model. It's perhaps most notable for the unmistakable, and dazzling presence of Chris Squire and Simon Phillips on bass and drums respectively. Delivered in a walking 6/8 time, Steve's singing brings Eric Clapton to mind, but the blistering soloing is all his – with perhaps a little stylistic help from Jimi Hendrix – with feedback, finger vibrato and sustain much in evidence.

'Turn This Island Earth' 11:51 (S. Hackett, J. Hackett, Howe, King, Mover)

The closing song is also the album's longest by some distance and one of

Steve's longest ever. The title is inspired by the 1955 sci-fi movie *This Island Earth* that Steve saw as a child and which has haunted him ever since. The words have a dream-like quality with numerous space exploration references that include the Milky Way and Rings of Saturn. Like 'Prairie Angel', it's another reworked track, leftover from the GTR period.

As you would expect, given the length, it's full of wonderful touches. The ominous intro perfectly captures the vastness and emptiness of space while the melodious vocal sequence at 7:00 boasts sumptuous harmonies. Squire and Phillips are once again in the engine room for the frantic instrumental bridge at 4:01. In 7/4 time, it's a sonic assault on a grand scale with keys strings and vibrant guitar jostling for attention. Elsewhere, King's inventive keyboard orchestrations have an epic sweep worthy of a film soundtrack. And that's without mentioning the triumphant hook of the chorus.

Related Tracks
The 'Special Edition' includes a bonus disc of nearly 30 minutes of additional material. Most of the nine tracks were leftovers from the *Beyond the Shrouded Horizon* sessions while others had been previously released. Typically, the Japanese release contains two extra tracks, recorded live during the *Out of the Tunnel's Mouth* tour. Both also appeared on the May 2011 *Live Rails* album.

'Four Winds: North' 1:35 (S. Hackett, King)
This is the first of four instrumentals inspired by the four winds which combine as a mini-suite. To represent the Boreas, we have an agreeable mid-tempo electric guitar workout backed by piano chords that fade all too soon.

'Four Winds: South' 2:06 (S. Hackett, King)
This is another short piece, this time for the Notos wind with fluid – and mostly improvised – piano and nylon guitar, which combine beautifully.

'Four Winds: East' 3:34 (S. Hackett, Benedict Fenner)
Representing Eurus, this track originally appeared on the Japanese edition of *Darktown* under the title 'The Well at the World's End'.

'Four Winds: West' 3:04 (S. Hackett, King)
Representing Zephyrus, this is a delightful nylon guitar solo with notes cascading like a waterfall. It previously appeared on Marco Lo Muscio's *The Book of Bilbo and Gandalf* album from 2010 under the title 'Galadriel'. Both Steve and John Hackett featured on that album.

'Pieds En L'Air' 2:26 (Peter Warlock)
Warlock – real name Philip Arnold Heseltine – was a British composer especially active in the 1920s. This was the fifth part of 'The Capriol Suite', a

set of six dances he wrote in 1926. An orchestral piece, it boasts a gorgeous string arrangement that's unashamedly romantic. It brings to mind vintage film composer Alfred Newman and his timeless score for the 1939 adaptation of *Wuthering Heights*.

'She Said Maybe' 4:21 (S. Hackett, King)

Roger King was chiefly responsible for this instrumental and here he demonstrates his flair for light jazz. He and Steve indulge in virtuoso synth and electric guitar exchanges to compelling effect, while King is also responsible for the rhythm track.

'Enter the Night' 4:00 (S. Hackett, J. Hackett, King)

A song that started life as the better known instrumental 'Riding the Colossus' – aka 'Depth Charge'. The playful, evocative words are inspired by J.M. Barries' *Peter Pan*. Despite Chris Squire's creative bass lines, I personally prefer the original instrumental version. Either way, it boasts one of Steve's most memorable tunes and was performed on the 2011 tour.

'Eruption: Tommy' 3:37 (Thijs van Leer)
'Reconditioned Nightmare' 4:06 (S. Hackett)

Both of these instrumentals previously appeared on the 2006 Japanese release of the *Wild Orchids* album – see earlier chapter.

'Fire on the Moon' (Live) 6:19 (S. Hackett)

The first of two additional tracks on the Japanese release of *Beyond the Shrouded Horizon*. The recording quality of both these live tracks is excellent. A song that works well on stage, this is a masterful performance that remains meticulously faithful to the studio version.

'Sleepers' (Live) 7:32 (S. Hackett, King, Jo Lehmann, Nick Clabburn)

This omits the lavish orchestral intro of the studio version and goes straight into the song part. Otherwise, it remains an extremely tight rendition with the whole band – especially saxophonist Rob Townsend – firing on all cylinders.

Genesis Revisited II (2012)

Personnel:

Steve Hackett: guitars, vocals on 'Supper's Ready – Willow Farm', 'Camino Royale'
Roger King: keyboards
Amanda Lehmann: guitar, vocals on 'Entangled', 'Ripples', 'Afterglow', 'Shadow of the Hierophant'
Jo Lehmann: backing vocals
Christine Townsend: violin, viola on 'The Chamber of 32 Doors', 'Can-Utility and the Coastliners', 'Blood on the Rooftops', 'A Tower Struck Down'
Dave Kerzner: additional keyboards on 'Supper's Ready'
Dick Driver: double bass on 'The Chamber of 32 Doors', 'Please Don't Touch', 'Blood on the Rooftops', 'A Tower Struck Down'
Francis Dunnery: guitar, vocals on 'Supper's Ready – As Sure As Eggs Is Eggs (Aching Men's Feet)', 'Dancing with the Moonlit Knight'
Gary O'Toole: drums, percussion, vocals
John Hackett: flute
John Wetton: bass, guitar, vocals on 'Afterglow'
Mikael Åkerfeldt: vocals on 'Supper's Ready – Lover's Leap', 'How Dare I Be So Beautiful?'
Nad Sylvan: vocals on 'The Chamber of 32 Doors', 'The Musical Box', 'Eleventh Earl of Mar'
Nik Kershaw: vocals on 'The Lamia'
Phil Mulford: bass on 'Blood on the Rooftops', 'Afterglow'
Rachel Ford: cello on 'The Chamber of 32 Doors', 'Blood on the Rooftops', 'A Tower Struck Down'
Roine Stolt: guitar on 'The Return of the Giant Hogweed'
Steve Rothery: guitar on 'The Lamia'
Nick Magnus: keyboards on 'Camino Royale'
Neal Morse: keyboards, vocals on 'The Return of the Giant Hogweed'
Jeremy Stacey: drums on 'Supper's Ready', 'Dancing with the Moonlit Knight'
Conrad Keely: vocals on 'Supper's Ready – Ikhnaton and Itsacon and Their Band of Merry Men'
Nick Beggs: bass, Chapman stick
Steven Wilson: guitar on 'Shadow of the Hierophant', vocals on 'Can-Utility and the Coastliners'
Rob Townsend: soprano and tenor saxophone, flute, whistle
Jakko Jakszyk: guitar, vocals on 'Entangled'
Simon Collins: keyboard, vocals on 'Supper's Ready – The Guaranteed Eternal Sanctuary Man', 'Apocalypse in 9/8'
Lee Pomeroy: bass, Chapman stick
Djabe: Ferenc Kovács: trumpet, violin, vocals. Attila Égerházi: guitar, percussion. Zoltán Kovács: piano, keyboards. Tamás Barabás: bass guitar. Szilárd Banai: drums on 'Camino Royale'
Produced by: Steve Hackett, Roger King

Recorded, mixed and mastered by: Roger King at Map Studios
Engineered by: Roger King, Alex Lyon, Benedict Fenner, Chris Frenchie Smith,
Dave Kerzner
Recording date: 2011 – 2012
Release date: 22 October 2012
Record label: Inside Out Music
Highest chart places: UK: 24, USA: Did not chart
Running time: 144:48

Following the success of *Genesis Revisited* in 1996, Steve decided to repeat
the formula with this aptly-titled two-disc successor. It was a not altogether
surprising move given that he maintains an affection for the songs and a good
deal of Genesis material had crept into his setlists of late. He also felt that
the latest recording technology and his contemporary guitar sound would
rejuvenate the music. Once again, it features a cast of thousands – well 33
at least – with several prominent names from the neo-neo prog world of the
1990s including Steven Wilson (Porcupine Tree), Roine Stolt (The Flower
Kings) and Neal Morse (ex Spock's Beard). Steve wasn't afraid of a little friendly
competition and the album boasts several excellent guitarists including Jakko
Jakszyk (soon to join King Crimson) and Steve Rothery (Marillion). Although
Chris Squire is absent, the Squackett collaboration *A Life Within a Day* had
been released earlier the same year.

As before, Steve sprinkles the album with a few of his own tunes which have
links – albeit tenuous – with Genesis, as he explains in the liner notes and
tracks are included from all six studio albums he played on between 1971 and
1977. *The Lamb Lies Down on Broadway* was virtually ignored on *Genesis
Revisited* and by way of compensation, four songs from the sprawling concept
are included on disc one. The epic 'Supper's Ready' also makes a welcome
appearance and disc two features a healthy selection from *Wind & Wuthering*.
The album's principal bassist Lee Pomeroy, who has a long association with
Rick Wakeman, toured with Steve in 2013.

Perhaps unsurprisingly, saleswise it was Steve's most successful UK album
since *Highly Strung* in 1983 and he also saw his first chart action since *Genesis
Revisited*. It entered the UK chart at 24 on 3 November 2012 where it stayed
for just one week. It also breached the top 100 in several European countries
and was certified gold in Japan. Fans generally praised the choice of material
and performances although dissenting voices amongst critics proves that you
can't please all of the people all of the time.

The subsequent 2013 – 2014 world tour was an unqualified success,
however, passing through Europe, the UK, Japan and North America.
It resulted in both *Genesis Revisited: Live at Hammersmith* released in
November 2013 and *Genesis Revisited: Live at the Royal Albert Hall* in July
2014. The albums were recorded just five months apart, a far cry from the
1970s when more than four years separated *Genesis Live* and *Seconds Out*.

The extensive CD booklet features a superb selection of photographs to represent each track, not least the simulated tidal wave engulfing St Mark's Basilica in Venice on the cover. The lyrics to every track, including the lengthy 'Supper's Ready' are included.

'The Chamber of 32 Doors' 6:00 (Tony Banks, Mike Rutherford, Peter Gabriel, Steve Hackett, Phil Collins)

This opener is the first of four tracks from the 1974 double LP concept *The Lamb Lies Down on Broadway,* regarded by many as Genesis' finest achievement. It's also the first of three songs featuring American-Swedish vocalist Nad Sylvan. Since the recording of this album, he has remained Steve's live singer for the *Genesis Revisited* shows and while it is a quality song, it's not an obvious album opener. Following a fleeting nylon guitar intro, Roger King perfectly recreates the string sound of the Mellotron Mark II, underscoring Steve's soaring guitar where the Fernandes sustainer pick-up goes into overdrive. Sylvan's malleable vocals swing effortlessly between the styles of Gabriel and Collins, often within a single verse.

'Horizons' 1:41 (Hackett)

Steve's best-known classical guitar piece gets yet another airing, and if anything this is a more gentle, less hurried version than previously recorded. The melody is influenced by the prelude to J.S. Bach's 'Cello Suite No. 1'.

'Supper's Ready' 23:35 (Banks, Rutherford, Gabriel, Hackett, Collins)

This is one of the seminal prog-rock epics of the 1970s and Genesis' finest hour – or rather half-hour – in this author's opinion. I was fortunate enough to witness Gabriel sing it in 1973 and Collins in 1976. It established the band as probably the most theatrical act of the early 1970s, both on record and on stage. Despite all the musical twists and turns and ambiguous lyrics, it boils down to a battle between good and evil and the former eventually triumphs.

Several singers are involved here, including Phil's son Simon Collins who sounds remarkably like his dad. The litmus test for any version of 'Supper's Ready' is the monumental 'Apocalypse in 9/8'. This version passes with flying colours with a stunning organ solo and the powerhouse rhythm engine of Lee Pomeroy (bass) and Jeremy Stacey (drums). The superb Francis Dunnery sings the emotive 'As Sure As Eggs Is Eggs' finale and, like the Genesis original, Steve's majestic solo fades all too soon.

'The Lamia' 7:47 (Banks, Rutherford, Gabriel, Hackett, Collins)

This is *The Lamb's* most romantic song in what is overall, essentially a mythological journey. Steve was especially drawn to this song because of the solo and he particularly liked Gabrel's poetic lyrics which stood out amongst

126

the urban angst displayed elsewhere. The golden-voiced Nik Kershaw is perfect for conveying the song's sensual undercurrent with sumptuous piano and flute from King and John Hackett respectively. The song's best part, the soaring guitar coda, doesn't disappoint with Steve and the excellent Steve Rothery supremely trading licks. Again, the dreaded fade arrives all too soon.

'Dancing with the Moonlit Knight' 8:10 (Banks, Rutherford, Gabriel, Hackett, Collins)

Steve's favourite Genesis track from his favourite Genesis album. He loves the strong melody and variety of styles including rock, folk, classical and jazz-fusion. There's a touch of Scottish plainsong and Elgar in the opening verses, Mozart influences in the Mellotron choir and a fast guitar riff worthy of Prokofiev. Steve's guitar soloing incorporates several trademark techniques including string tapping, sweet picking and octave jumps, driven by the propulsive jazz-rock drumming. In this version, he also incorporates a snippet of 'Greensleeves' at the beginning. Dunnery once again does the vocal honours.

'Fly on a Windshield' 2:54 (Banks, Rutherford, Gabriel, Hackett, Collins)

One of Steve's favourite songs from *The Lamb* is an atmospheric and powerful combination of guitar and Mellotron. The chord sequences reveal a classical influence from composers like Mussorgsky and Ravel and such influences were prevalent in a good deal of prog-rock in the 1970s. Musically, on the other hand, it evokes ancient Egypt and as a result, Genesis gave it the working title 'Pharaohs' when it was first recorded. Here, the thundering rhythm of Lee Pomeroy and Gary O'Toole underpin Hackett and King's howling interplay with suitably gothic results. It segues seamlessly into...

'Broadway Melody of 1974' 2:23 (Banks, Rutherford, Gabriel, Hackett, Collins)

Coming out from behind his drum kit, O'Toole delivers Gabriel's tongue-twisting lyrics in a sinister fashion, propelled by stabbing bass chords. Mellotron strings circle menacingly overhead and acoustic guitar is on hand for the tranquil conclusion.

'The Musical Box' 10:57 (Banks, Rutherford, Gabriel, Hackett, Collins)

This was the first song Steve recorded with Genesis in 1971. Typical of its time, it builds from gentle beginnings to epic crescendos. It showcased Gabriel's quirky, and very English lyrical style of combining Victorian gentility and eroticism. Additionally, Brain May later told Steve that he had been influenced by the three-part harmony guitar solo at the end of this song and the magisterial guitar tone is very identifiable as similar to 1970s Queen. At the risk of overstating the theme, Steve adds a musical box at the beginning,

Track*

but otherwise, this is a faithful version and an ideal vehicle for Sylvan's vocal talents. Rob Townsend adds delightful flute embellishments and the manic instrumental bolero bridge is, as always, a riot. The emotive 'Now, now, now, now' finale doesn't quite raise the hairs on the back of the neck like the original, but then you can't have everything!

'Can-Utility and the Coastliners' 5:50 (Banks, Rutherford, Gabriel, Hackett, Collins)

Opening with finger cymbals and pastoral twelve-string guitar, Steve was originally responsible for writing the vocal part of this song. Although Genesis initially played it on the 1972 tour in Italy before the release of *Foxtrot*, it was a difficult track to nail live and was soon dropped from the set. It remains one of Genesis' most underrated tunes, and this is perhaps the most successful re-interpretation on the album. Steven Wilson provides a suitably sensitive vocal, but the track belongs to Roger King with magisterial Hammond-like organ and Mellotron string samples of symphonic proportions. Towards the end, the stumbling, rhythmic Mellotron part with jazz-like drumming and the guitar jam is simply stunning.

'Please Don't Touch' 4:03 (Hackett)

As discussed previously, Steve pitched this instrumental to Genesis in 1976 for the *Wind & Wuthering* album, but it lost out to Phil Collins' 'Wot Gorilla?'. It was reworked for 'Unquiet Slumbers for the Sleepers' which appears on disc two here. This track closes disc one and to my ears, it improves on the 1978 original. While retaining the gothic urgency, King's lush orchestrations lend an added majesty while Steve's scorching guitar and John's lively flute are a match made in heaven.

'Blood on the Rooftops' 6:56 (Hackett, Collins)

Back in 1976, Steve suggested a classical guitar intro to this song which appealed to the other members of Genesis. It's very English in subject and Steve's lyrics about a father and son watching TV include references to shows popular in the 1970s. In the chorus, the father finds it hard to watch the current news events, still recalling the harsh realities of the second world war. An extended nylon guitar solo sets the scene, and once again O'Toole steps up to the microphone for this song, something which he would repeat on stage many times. Add piano, chiming percussion, a string quartet and Townsend's soprano sax and you have a superb version of probably Steve's finest contribution to any Genesis album.

'The Return of the Giant Hogweed' 8:46 (Banks, Rutherford, Gabriel, Hackett, Collins)

This is a song based on a newspaper article that Peter Gabriel read about a plant that disappeared from London's Kew Gardens. It was also influenced by the book and film *The Day of the Triffids*. Steve was responsible for the 'The Return of' part of the title to suggest a film sequel. Both musically and lyrically it's quintessentially English and early Genesis.

The multi-talented Neal Morse and Roine Stolt have occasionally included Genesis songs in their repertoires and here they provide vocals and keyboards and guitar respectively. Stolt guested on this song at the Royal Albert Hall in October 2013 and was a member of Steve's touring band in 2015. Steve had also played the track with the pair's supergroup Transatlantic at the High Voltage Festival in the UK in July 2010. It's out of the starting gate like a thoroughbred with Steve's guitar tapping to the fore and Morse singing with much gusto. John adds a gutsy flute solo at the halfway mark and the instrumental bridge is extended to accommodate Stolt's bluesy guitar shredding. The frenzied instrumental finale remains the best part, however, with everyone firing on all cylinders.

'Entangled' 6:35 (Hackett, Banks)

Another personal favourite, this exquisite song featured on *A Trick of the Tail* and is a rare writing partnership between the guitarist and keyboardist. When Steve wrote the lyrics, he imagined a psychiatrist hypnotising a patient and transporting him back into a world of troubled dreams. Banks was responsible for the chorus. The counterpointing, chiming acoustic guitars that ground the song are very characteristic of 1970's Genesis. Multi-instrumentalist Jakko Jakszyk provides the vocals and his harmonising with Amanda Lehmann during the chorus is sheer perfection. Once again, King does a brilliant job of duplicating Banks' keyboard parts with eerie synth underpinning the ghostly Mellotron choir for the spine-tingling coda.

'Eleventh Earl of Mar' 7:51 (Banks, Hackett, Rutherford)

When this track was recorded, Steve and Jo had recently visited Braemar Castle in Scotland, where the story is set. It's a fine example of Genesis' storytelling style and although it was mostly group written, Steve was responsible for the infectious organ riff and the bridge section which he retrieved from another song. It still works well in a live setting as he proved on the *Wind & Wuthering* 40th anniversary tour. The synth, guitar and Mellotron crescendo at the beginning is sublime, harking back to 'The Fountain of Salmacis' on *Nursery Cryme*. Nad Sylvan probably provides his most passionate vocal on the album, matching Collins note for note. The additional counterpoint harmonies during the tranquil bridge at 4:00 are beautiful and Steve provides three-part harmony guitar for the majestic finale which brings the song back to its opening theme.

'Ripples' 8:14 (Rutherford, Banks)

This is another characteristic Genesis song with twelve-string guitar and superb musical dynamics, contrasting light and shade. It's Amanda's moment to shine, providing the evocative lead vocals with gorgeous multi-tracked harmonies during the chorus. When she sings 'Sail away' one thinks of Enya's 'Orinoco Flow' – same words but a completely different tune, of course. It's the instrumental bridge that remains at the song's heart however, with synth, piano and swirling guitar – with the beginning of the note cut-off to make it sound like it's played backwards – that reach grandiose heights. Amanda sang an acoustic version of 'Ripples' in 2013 during the extended *Genesis Revisited II* tour with the instrumental section removed.

'Unquiet Slumbers for the Sleepers...' 2:12 (Hackett, Rutherford)
The final three Genesis tracks replicate the conclusion to the *Wind & Wuthering* album. The title of this, and the following linked instrumental, will be familiar to anyone that has read Emily Brontë's *Wuthering Heights.* Staying close to the original, it's darkly atmospheric, conjuring up images of the novel's setting on the wind-swept Yorkshire moors, shrouded in mist.

'...In That Quiet Earth' 4:47 (Hackett, Rutherford, Banks, Collins)
This, on the other hand, hits the ground running, allowing Steve, Beggs, O'Toole, King and Townsend the opportunity to flex their considerable musical muscles. Genesis really should have written more instrumentals – it's tuneful and brilliantly performed, what more could you ask? It flows beautifully into...

'Afterglow' 4:09 (Banks)
This is a strong contender for Tony Banks' best ever song – whether in Genesis or as a solo artist. It's a compelling ballad where the chorus is hardly discernible from the verses and it doesn't get much better than this. Driven by ringing guitar chords, the stately rhythm could have very easily sounded plodding in the wrong hands, but this version treats the original with the utmost respect, right down to the layered, wordless harmonies during the coda. John Wetton gives a fine, emotional performance even though it stretches him to the upper limits of his vocal range.

'A Tower Struck Down' 4:45 (John Hackett, Steve Hackett)
This is the first of three non-Genesis tracks to close the album and it was originally performed with Rutherford and Collins on Steve's *Voyage of the Acolyte* album. Here, the Led Zep-like rhythmic stomp is sweetened by strings that would not sound out of place on the soundtrack to an Alfred Hitchcock thriller. Elsewhere, however, it maintains the aggressive tone of the original.

'Camino Royale' 6:19 (Steve Hackett, Nick Magnus)
This song opened Steve's 1983 *Highly Strung* album and it's one that he believed would have suited Genesis. It has links with the New Orleans jazz sound and Genesis at their most free-spirited. Keyboardist Nick Magnus, who first worked with Steve back in 1978 plays a big part in creating the sounds on

this version as does Hungarian band Djabe with whom Steve performed on several occasions. Bordering on jazz-fusion, the piece swings from intense to mellow and back again. The musicianship is stunning.

'Shadow of the Hierophant' 10:45 (Hackett, Rutherford)

As this was co-written with the Genesis bassist for potential inclusion on the 1972 *Foxtrot* album, Steve felt justified to include it here. As well as Amanda's beautiful singing during the introductory song section, this version is notable for the guitar work of Steven Wilson. Rob Townsend provides delightful flute accompaniment to the vocal and Steve's weeping guitar has rarely sounded sweeter. The near six-minute instrumental finale builds from tranquil beginnings to an apocalyptic climax – rather than the less satisfying fade of the original.

Related Tracks

An abridged version of the album entitled *Genesis Revisited II: Selection* was released in May 2013. It includes eight songs from the original album, plus a previously unreleased version of 'Carpet Crawlers'.

'Carpet Crawlers' 5:12 (Banks, Collins, Gabriel, Hackett, Rutherford)

Ray Wilson first sang this song on tour with Genesis after he joined as a replacement for Phil Collins in 1996. He has also performed it live with Steve in more recent times. Here, he gives a creditable performance with call and response vocals that's more Gabriel than Collins, perfectly in tune with the song's haunting, dream-like ambience. King's shimmering keys and Steve's plaintive guitar play their part in the song's slow-burning build.

'All Along The Watchtower' 4:42 (Bob Dylan)

Steve's second cover of a Dylan song was recorded in 2013 as a bonus track for Esoteric Recordings' 2CD/DVD reissue of *The Tokyo Tapes*. Prior to this studio recording, Steve and John Wetton had performed it together on stage. Steve's bluesy guitar and Wetton's earthy vocal – supported by King, Pomeroy and O' Toole – capture the spirit of Jimi Hendrix's legendary version.

Wolflight (2015)

Personnel:
Steve Hackett: guitars, banjo, oud, tiple, harmonica, percussion, lead, harmony and backing vocals
Roger King: keyboards, programming
Nick Beggs: bass on all tracks except 'Love Song to a Vampire', Chapman Stick on 'Black Thunder'
Chris Squire: bass on 'Love Song to a Vampire'
Gary O'Toole: drums on 'Out of the Body' to 'Corycian Fire', 'Black Thunder'
Hugo Degenhardt: drums on 'Dust and Dreams', 'Heart Song'
Rob Townsend: sax on 'The Wheel's Turning', 'Black Thunder', duduk on 'Corycian Fire'
Christine Townsend: violin, viola on 'Out of the Body' to 'The Wheel's Turning', 'Black Thunder'
Amanda Lehmann: vocals on 'Wolflight' to 'The Wheel's Turning', 'Black Thunder'
Joanna Hackett: vocals on 'The Wheel's Turning'
Malik Mansurov: tar on 'Wolflight'
Sara Kovács: didgeridoo on 'Wolflight'
Produced by: Steve Hackett, Roger King
Recorded, mixed and mastered by: Roger King at Map Studios
Recording date: 2012 – 2014
Release date: 27 March 2015
Record label: Inside Out Music / Century Media
Highest chart places: UK: 31, USA: Did not chart
Running time: 55:31

With the successful *Genesis Revisited* world tour stretching well into 2015 with dates in South America, work on Steve's 23rd studio album became somewhat protracted. Following the extravagance of *Genesis Revisited II*, the recording sessions for this album were more modest with his live band performing on the majority of the tracks. Thanks to the tour raising his profile, sales for *Wolflight* were healthy, entering the UK chart at 31 on 11 April 2015, where it stayed for one week. It also made the top 50 in several European regions. Despite the absence of brother John, several International guest musicians play on the title song and the bonus track 'Midnight Sun'.

According to Steve's liner notes, the album has the title it does because much of it was written in 'wolf light', the hour before dawn when these predatory animals like to hunt. Once again, it's a musical travelogue, influenced in part by the twenty countries Steve visited during the tour. *Wolflight* was simultaneously released on vinyl, CD, Blu-ray and digital download.

'Love Song to a Vampire' was the last recording made by Chris Squire. On 19 May 2015, it was announced that he had been diagnosed with acute erythroid leukaemia and despite undergoing treatment, he passed away on 27 June. The groundbreaking bassist was the only member of Yes to play on every single one of their albums and he is still much missed.

Wolflight was launched in Germany with fan preview events in Dortmund and Berlin on 27 and 28 March 2015 respectively. 2015 was the 40th anniversary of Steve's debut album and the *Acolyte to Wolflight with Genesis Classics* tour crossed East and West Europe and the UK from July to October and America in November and December. The resulting album *The Total Experience Live in Liverpool* was recorded on 23 October and released the following June. The setlist typically featured solo material in the first half and Genesis in the second with 'Clocks' and 'Firth of Fifth' often providing the encore.

The North American leg continued in March 2016 including dates in Canada followed by a trip to Japan in May. On 22 May, Steve co-headlined the Tokyo Progressive Rock Festival with Camel and on 19 June, he shared the bill at London's Stone Free Festival with Rick Wakeman and Marillion. To round off a busy year, Steve, Roger King and Rob Townsend embarked on the *2016 Acoustic Trio Italian Tour* in July.

Maurizio and Angéla Vicedomini are responsible for the excellent photo montage in the CD booklet which, like *Genesis Revisited II*, features a separate image to represent each song. The photo composite on the cover depicts Steve and a friendly pack of wolves in a nighttime setting, appropriate for these nocturnal predators. They were, in fact, tame wolves that Steve and his partner Jo visited one day during a trip to Italy.

'Out of the Body' 2:29 (Steve Hackett)
Despite Steve's repertoire dominated by Genesis songs and his own earlier classics, the subsequent tour featured between five and six songs from *Wolflight*, including this opening track. The others regularly played were 'Wolflight', 'Love Song to a Vampire', 'The Wheel's Turning', 'Corycian Fire' and 'Loving Sea'. It also features on the live albums *The Total Experience Live in Liverpool* and *Genesis Revisited Band & Orchestra: Live at the Royal Festival Hall*.

Opening with the sampled sounds of a baying animal and birdsong, this is a vibrant instrumental with a strong theme that establishes the overall mood of the album. It piles on the instrumental layers with real strings and keyboard orchestrations complementing the electric guitar harmonics. The mid-section is particularly melodramatic and the track ends with a classical guitar flourish.

'Wolflight' 8:00 (Steve Hackett, Jo Hackett)
The title song is one of Steve's most ambitious with a multi-faceted arrangement that goes through numerous changes. It was inspired by the grey wolves – as pictured on the album cover – that wander the Italian Peninsula. The lyrics relate to the nomads who share the same land where travel is integral to their existence, while the core melody bears a similarity to 'Fire on the Moon' that opened the *Out of the Tunnel's Mouth* album.

Once again, Roger King's virtual orchestra is at the heart of the piece, while Steve indulges in a variety of guitar textures including acoustic-folk, classical and aggressive electric soloing to depict the harsh way of life. This is captured in a beautifully shot, eight-minute video to promote the album, which was filmed around the mountains of Serbia. For the choral harmonies, Steve is joined by Amanda Lehmann while Gary O'Toole is responsible for the powerful tribal drumming. The tar hand drum and didgeridoo, played by Malik Mansurov and Sara Kovács respectively, were recorded at Grammy Studio, Budapest by Tamas Barabas.

'Love Song to a Vampire' 9:18 (S. Hackett)

Another long song, this is not to be confused with 'Love Song for a Vampire' written and sung by Annie Lennox for Francis Ford Coppola's 1992 film *Bram Stoker's Dracula*. They share similar traits, however, and this particular song is dedicated to a certain type of self-serving person who uses their charm and charisma to exert their power and will over others. This is another song that benefitted from a promotional video with high production values.

To set the scene, Steve opens with a flamenco guitar solo followed by an ornate vocal sequence. The soaring choral hook kicks in for the first time at 2:10 and it's a strong one, contrasting with the brooding verses. Steve combines two guitar tracks – one edgy, one melodic – for the instrumental bridge while Chris Squire provides the rising bass line. He just happened to be in London for a few days and he asked Steve if he had anything he could be involved with. The deep down and dirty guitar solo at 7:57 is pure heavy metal, but nylon guitar returns just in time for the tranquil conclusion.

'The Wheel's Turning' 7:24 (S. Hackett, J. Hackett, Roger King)

This song is a return to Steve's childhood and London's Battersea funfair that he frequented in the 1960s. Although the song is a nostalgic trip down memory lane with fond memories for Steve, some years later the fair was the scene of the worst roller coaster accident in UK history. On 30 May 1972, five children died on 'The Big Dipper' which was subsequently closed down, as was the fair two years later.

Appropriately, the song opens and closes with the sound of a fairground organ. In keeping with the period, the vocal part with its catchy chorus incorporates Beatles, Beach Boys and Roy Orbison influences. The instrumental histrionics are all Steve and Roger's, however, utilising energetic guitar volleys, harmonica and distorted programmed strings to replicate the exhilaration of the various rides. The lush symphonic interlude at 4:55 is pure Tchaikovsky.

'Corycian Fire' 5:47 (S. Hackett, J. Hackett, King)

This song was inspired by a visit to the Corycian Cave located on the slopes of Mount Parnassus, in central Greece. The location is steeped in ancient Greek myths and Steve tells of ancient rituals held in the cave to bring the god

Dionysus back to life. An imaginative video for this song features a routine performed by dancers filmed in Greece and the UK, while musically, there are echoes of Hans Zimmer and Lisa Gerrard's award-winning film score for *Gladiator.*

For the atmospheric intro, Rob Townsend plays a duduk wind instrument backed by harp which gives the song an authentic, Mediterranean flavour. Steve plays the oud, a lute-type stringed instrument. His wistful vocal is supported by King's sweet strings before the song explodes into life at 1:22. Here, the vocals are heavily processed with O'Toole and Nick Beggs maintaining a tight rhythmic grip and the hyperactive instrumental section at 3:45 is worthy of Genesis at their best. It concludes with a stunning choral sequence sung in Greek that recalls Carl Orff's 'Carmina Burana' with a rhythm, however, that suggests Steve's 'A Tower Struck Down'.

'Earthshine' 3:20 (S. Hackett)
By way of a respite from all the melodrama, Steve slots in the almost obligatory nylon guitar instrumental. It's a warm, uplifting piece played with plenty of verve, incorporating classical, jazz and flamenco textures.

'Loving Sea' 3:22 (S. Hackett, J. Hackett)
With its sparse arrangement of ringing acoustic guitar and multi-tracked harmonies for both the verses and chorus, this song more than hints at Crosby, Stills, Nash & Young. Steve plays a tiple guitar and there is also a hint of sitar and backward electric guitar in the mix. It has an infectious, feelgood factor that sets it apart from anything else on the album, so this track should be filed in the same category as Stephen Stills' 'Love the One You're With'. The song was inspired by Steve and Jo's visit to a remote lagoon in Mexico and relates to the wonders of the sea and its surrounding wildlife.

'Black Thunder' 7:32 (S. Hackett, J. Hackett)
Steve felt compelled to write this song following an emotional sabbatical to the former home of Martin Luther King in Atlanta, Georgia. The song 'Freedom' by Richie Havens also played a part in this story of a slave rebellion in America's deep south, so the song's subject is similar to that of 'Underground Railroad' on *At the Edge of Light.* To set the scene, it opens with dobro-like acoustic guitar, banjo and violin. From here on, we're in mid-tempo, hard rock territory with stinging guitar chords, sledgehammer drums, blues-harp and spiky guitar soloing. There are several sweeteners along the way, however, including King's lush orchestrations, rich choral work and Beggs' Chapman Stick break. Townsend has the final word with an evocative soprano sax solo.

'Dust and Dreams' 5:33 (S. Hackett, King)
The Arabian sounds in this instrumental were inspired by a visit to Morocco on

the edge of the Sahara desert where Steve was enchanted by the local music he heard. It has a laid-back, cool jazz vibe with a skipping rhythm and guitar and keys gently ebbing and flowing. At 3:20, it elevates into more dramatic territory although the guitar remains firmly on the melodic side of neutral. The prominent, staccato riff – before the track comes to an abrupt stop – owes an obvious debt to Jimmy Page.

'Heart Song' 2:51 (S. Hackett)
There's no connection between this closing song and Gordon Giltrap's much loved 1977 instrumental 'Heartsong'. Instead, it's an unabashed love song dedicated to Steve's soulmate, Jo. Although I feel I should like it more, this for me is one of his weakest offerings. The laid-back arrangement does offer a few incentives, however, such as soaring guitar breaks, Hugo Degenhardt's restrained drumming and ringing guitar chords that hark back to Genesis' 'Afterglow'. The vocal melody, however, has a touch of cloying tweeness about it.

Related Tracks
The double LP vinyl version includes three extra tracks absent from the standard CD – 'Pneuma', 'Midnight Sun' and 'Caress'. These occupy side four. A special edition CD includes 'Pneuma' and 'Midnight Sun' plus a Blu-ray disc featuring a 5.1 surround sound mix of the album. The Blu-ray also contains the video extras 'Steve Hackett discusses recording Wolflight' (7:00), 'Steve Hackett discusses Wolflight artwork', (7:18) and 'Wolflight track-by-track' (31:24).

'Pneuma' 2:52 (S. Hackett)
'Pneuma' is an ancient Greek word for 'breath' and – in a religious context – 'soul' and 'spirit'. Another excellent nylon guitar solo, and despite sounding more Spanish than Greek, it radiates a genuine warmth.

'Midnight Sun' 4:32 (Thorvaldur B Thorvaldsson, S. Hackett)
Recorded with Icelandic rock group Todmobile, this song is both personal for Steve and evocative of the dramatic landscapes of Iceland. It has an engaging folk-rock vibe and a striking melody that owes more to Todmobile than it does Steve with excellent lead vocals from Eythor Ingi Gunnlaugsson. It appeared on their 2014 album *Úlfur* which features Steve on guitar and Jon Anderson of Yes on vocals.

'Caress' 4:40 (S. Hackett)
This is indeed a suitable title as this classical guitar instrumental reaches out to the listener and holds them in a warm embrace. Steve utilises his wonderful technique of plucking the upper and lower strings to simulate the sound of two guitars playing in unison.

'Unspoken' 1:30 (Leslie-Miriam Bennet, Benedict Fenner)
A bonus track only on the Japanese edition of *Wolflight*. This is a melancholic instrumental with moody electric guitar overlayed on opulent keyboard orchestrations courtesy of Ben Fenner and his partner Leslie Bennet.

The Night Siren (2017)

Personnel:
Steve Hackett: electric and acoustic guitars, oud, charango, sitar guitar, harmonica, vocals
Kobi Farhi: vocals on 'West to East'
Mīrā 'Awaḍ: vocals on 'West to East'
Nick D'Virgilio: drums on 'Martian Sea'
Malik Mansurov: tar on 'Behind the Smoke'
Gulli Briem: drums, Cajon, percussion on 'Inca Terra', 'In the Skeleton Gallery'
Roger King: keyboards, programming (except on 'The Gift')
Benedict Fenner: keyboards, programming on 'The Gift'
Leslie-Miriam Bennett: keyboards on 'The Gift'
Nad Sylvan: vocals on 'Inca Terra'
Jo Hackett: vocals on 'West to East'
Gary O'Toole: drums on 'Fifty Miles from the North Pole', 'El Niño', 'West to East'
Rob Townsend: baritone saxophone, soprano saxophone, flute, flageolet, quena, duduk, bass clarinet
Amanda Lehmann: vocals
Christine Townsend: violin, viola
Dick Driver: double bass
Troy Donockley: uilleann pipes on 'In Another Life'
John Hackett: flute on 'Martian Sea', 'West to East'
Ferenc Kovács: trumpet on 'Fifty Miles from the North Pole'
Sara Kovács: didgeridoo on 'Fifty Miles from the North Pole'
Produced by Steve Hackett, Roger King, Benedict Fenner
Recorded and mixed by: Roger King at Siren and Benedict Fenner at The Paddock ('The Gift')
Engineered by Roger King, Benedict Fenner, Duncan Parsons, Mark Hornsby, Tamas Barabas
Recording date: 2014 – 2017
Release date: 24 March 2017
Record label: Inside Out Music
Highest chart places: UK: 28, USA: Did not chart
Running time: 57:40

The Night Siren was released exactly two years after its predecessor, no mean feat given the lengthy touring in between. Like *Wolflight*, the album was released in multiple formats although this time the double LP and single CD feature the same tracks. Typically, the Japanese edition includes two bonus tracks. The extensive touring certainly paid off, the album reaching 28 in the UK chart on 6 April 2017 and it did good business in several European countries. Despite touring the USA immediately prior to the album's release, Steve once again disappointingly failed to chart in that region.

Steve and Jo's globe-trotting was again a major influence with several tracks adopting world music stylings thanks to multicultural artists from regions like Asia and the Middle East bringing a variety of ethnic instrumentation to the table. As was now becoming common practice, several of the performers, like Nick D'Virgilio and Malik Mansurov, were recorded in different locations including America, Budapest and Sardinia. They were then added to the overall mix in London by Roger King.

To promote the album, Steve and his band embarked on the *Genesis Revisited with Classic Hackett* 2017 tour with the emphasis on *Wind & Wuthering* to mark that album's 40th anniversary. Following appearances at the *Giants of Rock* UK festival in January 2017 and *Cruise to the Edge* 2017 on 'MS Brilliance of the Seas' in February, the tour covered North America, Europe, the UK, Ireland, New Zealand and Australia. Genesis material dominated, with only a handful of 'Classic Hackett' songs in the set. On the back of the tour, *Wuthering Nights: Live in Birmingham,* recorded in May, was released the following January.

Maurizio and Angéla Vicedomini were once again responsible for the artwork of the new album. Photos were compiled from exotic locations around the world to represent each of the eleven tracks. The cover image – of the northern lights – was also reproduced in part on the vinyl LP labels.

'Behind the Smoke' 6:57 (Steve Hackett, Jo Hackett, Roger King)

This is a philosophical opener that looks back to the roots of mankind and the rocky road that faced our ancestors. The song also has a contemporary setting that concerns the plight of refugees escaping their own troubled situation, a topic close to Steve's heart. Jo was responsible for the subject and the opening line that contains the song title.

The plaintive verses feature harp and Steve's vocal sounding more natural than usual, with no obvious processing or multi-tracking. He cites American singer Tim Rose as an influence on this album and there's certainly a similarity with his down to earth vocal style here. The song hits its rhythmic stride at 1:15 with a powerful orchestrated riff, a technique that Steve and Roger King had by now made their own. Edgy guitar soloing whips up the tension and the symphonic instrumental bridge at the halfway mark brings a touch of Rachmaninoff – perhaps by way of famed film composer John Williams – to the table. King is also responsible for the virtual drum solo at 4:50. Steve really enjoyed playing this song live, where the insistent riff really came into its own. Along with 'El Niño' and 'In the Skeleton Gallery', it was one of only three songs played with any regularity on the subsequent 2017 and 2018 tours.

'Martian Sea' 4:40 (S. Hackett, King)

Compared with the previous track, this piece is delivered at a breathless pace with Nick D'Virgilio's relentless drumming doing well to maintain pace with the hyperactive vocal track. Everyone takes a breather at 2:42 for the instrumental coda which takes a psychedelic turn with orchestral keys joined by John Hackett's flute, backwards guitar and electric sitar. The song title – and memorable choral hook – refers to the scientific theory that the red planet was once partly covered by an ocean. The lyrics, however, are about alienation and tell of an obsessive relationship gone sour with lines like 'You said one day you'd ruin me if I ever tried to leave'.

'Fifty Miles from the North Pole' 7:08 (S. Hackett, J. Hackett, Amanda Lehmann)

This is a song inspired by two live shows in Iceland by Steve and his band, one of which was 50 miles from the Arctic Circle. As such, the title is a little misleading as in reality, Iceland is more than 3,000 miles from the North Pole. He had also got to know Icelandic rock band Todmobile and occasionally performed with them.

Musically, it's another song with something of an identity crisis that's mellow, cool jazz one moment and full-on, riff-driven rock the next. The twangy guitar in the former section sounds like it's wandered in on route to the latest Bond movie. Meanwhile, the sweet harmonies at 1:23 could give the Beach Boys a run for their money while a multi-tracked Amanda Lehmann provides the exotic choral sequence. The instrumentation is equally rich including Ferenc Kovács' trumpet, Sara Kovács' didgeridoo and real strings courtesy of Christine Townsend and Dick Driver. The song's highpoint with soaring guitar, driven by an infectious bolero rhythm, lasts for all of thirteen seconds.

'El Niño' 3:51 (S. Hackett, King)

The title of this instrumental and the music references the natural phenomenon that warms the oceans water. It can disrupt weather patterns with potentially devastating consequences across several continents. Dramatic strings – à la *Jeff Wayne's Musical Version of The War of the Worlds* – provide the introduction and punctuate the music as it storms along like a tornado. Gary O'Toole is responsible for the whirlwind drumming, while the frantic guitar riffs at 1:09 and 2:05 recall 'A Tower Struck Down' from over 40 years earlier.

'Other Side of the Wall' 4:00 (S. Hackett, J. Hackett)

Nylon guitar makes its album debut here, introducing this tranquil song with Steve in romantic vocal mode. A change of key at 1:33 and jangling twelve-string guitar takes up the cause with a transition to a memorable middle-eight. Relating to an imaginary forbidden love, the song was inspired by Steve and Jo's discovery of an abandoned walled garden in Wimbledon, London that conjured up images of the secrets it may hold. The song has a delicate intimacy that recalls early Genesis at their best. The counterpoint harmonies are to die for before concluding with a symphonic flourish of strings and choral voices that soar skywards. Steve's singing has rarely sounded better and this is another strong contender for his list of most underrated songs.

'Anything but Love' 5:56 (S. Hackett)

Lively flamenco guitar and a foot-tapping rhythm send this song dancing across your living room before it settles into a catchy, mid-tempo groove. Steve and Amanda share lead vocals – something they ought to do more often – dueting brilliantly for the melodious chorus. It's a story of infatuation and unrequited love and Steve accents the frustration in such a relationship with a blues-harp solo and a gutsy guitar workout at 3:26. It's one of his longest solos on record and the song ends in a barely-controlled wall of inspired cacophony.

'Inca Terra' 5:53 (S. Hackett, J. Hackett)

Nad Sylvan had become the touring singer to interpret the Genesis songs and here he makes his studio debut on an original Hackett song. Singing in harmony with Steve and Amanda, his enigmatic tones are almost unrecognisable. An evocative folk-rock song, it was influenced by another of Steve's many travels, this time Peru's tropical Cloud Forest on the slopes of the Andes. The instrumental bridge at 1:34 brings to mind the Peruvian tune 'El Cóndor Pasa' – made famous by Simon & Garfunkel – thanks to Rob Townsend's woodwind, some mandolin-like guitar and a basic rhythm. It morphs into an intricate, wordless choral sequence backed by acoustic guitar that recalls 1960's folk-harmony groups like The Settlers and The Swingle Singers. At 3:00, it kicks up its heels for an extended instrumental sequence with Steve's soaring guitar, driven by Gunnlaugur Briem's energetic and masterful drumming.

'In Another Life' 6:07 (S. Hackett, J. Hackett, King, Troy Donockley)

A song set in Scotland's troubled past, this piece has a strong affinity with films like *Highlander* and *Braveheart,* recalling tales of bloody battles and the tyranny of English oppression. Appropriately, the vocal sequence evokes Scottish plainsong with Steve's three-part harmonies supported by Amanda's velvet tones. The instrumental bridge provides the musical soundtrack to the story with Steve's expressive guitar solo charting the trials and tribulations of the protagonists. The song's highpoint, however, comes at 5:00 with a haunting uilleann pipes melody courtesy of the brilliant Troy Donockley, underpinned by King's orchestral keys. Although the uilleann pipes are normally associated with Ireland rather than Scotland, the instrument's timeless quality is a worthy substitute for the bagpipes.

'In the Skeleton Gallery' 5:09 (S. Hackett, J. Hackett)

This song was originally released as a download on 4 February 2017 as a taster for the album. It looks back to Steve's childhood and – like so my children – the nightmares, dreams and fantasies he experienced from his active imagination. The melody was written by Jo, and appropriately it has a dreamy, psychedelic vibe complete with backwards guitar and Briem's relaxed drum shuffle. The Hackett-Lehmann vocal harmonies are once again heavenly and at 1:48 and 3:45, Townsend lets fly with terrific soprano sax solos. At 2:50, King's

Mellotron samples introduce heavy guitar and bass chords, before a child's musical box seizes back the theme for the gentle conclusion.

'West to East' 5:14 (S. Hackett, J. Hackett)

This is a song that calls for compassion and unity with an optimistic message telling us that opposing nations and ideals can coexist. To underline the sentiment, two of the singers here – Kobi Farhi and Mīrā 'Awaḍ – have Israeli and Palestinian links. For the chorus, Jo makes a rare vocal appearance along with her sister Amanda.

Like the previous track, the verses have a dream-like quality, supplemented by a rousing choral hook that has an arm-waving, feelgood character. Like 'Heart Song' on *Wolflight*, the ringing rhythm guitar recalls Genesis' 'Afterglow'. Appropriately, the soaring instrumental bridge at 2:51 mixes western and eastern styles with Steve's melodic guitar accompanied by John's flute and sweet strings. Under the right conditions in a different time, an edited version of this song would have made a superb single.

'The Gift' 2:45 (Leslie-Miriam Bennet, Benedict Fenner)

The closing track is a melancholic instrumental with the composers providing an orchestral keyboards backdrop to Steve's serenading guitar. If the instrument's full-bodied tone brings Gary Moore to mind, that's because it's a Fernandes model that once belonged to him before Steve acquired it.

Related Tracks

In addition to the vinyl and CD versions, a 'Special Edition' CD and Blu-ray package was released. The latter featured a 5.1 surround sound mix of the album and 'Somewhere in Darkest Teddington – The Recording of The Night Siren' documentary directed by Paul Gosling. The Japanese CD features two bonus tracks, 'After the Ordeal' and 'Jazz on a Summer's Night'.

'After the Ordeal' 6:46 (Tony Banks, Phil Collins, Peter Gabriel, Steve Hackett, Mike Rutherford)

Although credited to the entire band at the time, this atmospheric instrumental was written by Steve with input from Mike and Tony and has been disparaged by the latter ever since. The title reflects that it immediately follows 'The Battle of Epping Forest' on the *Selling England by the Pound* album. A track of two halves, this version opens with Steve and Roger's complex classical guitar and piano duet followed by an extended weeping electric guitar solo that was a duet with Roine Stolt on *The Total Experience Live in Liverpool*.

'Jazz on a Summer's Night' 3:03 (S. Hackett)

More classical with a touch of folk than jazz, this is a beautifully nimble duet featuring acoustic guitar and flute courtesy of Steve and John.

At the Edge of Light (2019)

Personnel:
Steve Hackett: electric, acoustic & twelve-string guitars, dobro, bass guitar, harmonica, vocals
Durga McBroom & Lorelei McBroom: vocals on 'Underground Railroad'
Nick D'Virgilio: drums on 'Those Golden Wings'
Simon Phillips: drums on 'Hungry Years'
Sheema Mukherjee: sitar on 'Shadow and Flame'
Malik Mansurov: tar on 'Fallen Walls and Pedestals'
Jonas Reingold: bass guitar on 'Beasts in Our Time', 'Under the Eye of the Sun', 'Hungry Years'
Paul Stillwell: didgeridoo on 'Under the Eye of the Sun'
Gulli Briem: drums, percussion on 'Under the Eye of the Sun'
Rob Townsend: tenor saxophone, flute, duduk, bass clarinet on 'Beasts in Our Time', 'Under the Eye of the Sun'
Amanda Lehmann: vocals on 'Under the Eye of the Sun', 'Underground Railroad', 'Those Golden Wings', 'Hungry Years', 'Peace'
John Hackett: flute on 'Beasts in Our Time', 'Under the Eye of the Sun', 'Those Golden Wings', 'Conflict'
Gary O'Toole: drums on 'Fallen Walls and Pedestals'
Roger King: keyboards, programming, orchestral arrangements (except on 'Descent')
Benedict Fenner: keyboards, programming on 'Hungry Years', 'Descent'
Dick Driver: double bass on 'Under the Eye of the Sun', 'Those Golden Wings'
Christine Townsend: violin, viola on 'Those Golden Wings'
Produced by Steve Hackett, Roger King, Benedict Fenner
Engineered by Roger King, Benedict Fenner
Recorded and mixed by: Roger King at Siren (except 'Decent') and Benedict Fenner at The Paddock ('Decent')
Recording date: 2018
Release date: 25 January 2019
Record label: InsideOut Music
Highest chart places: UK: 28, USA: Did not chart
Running time: 54:27

Steve's 25th studio album is probably also his most ambitious with a scope that's almost conceptual in structure. While it's musically diverse, it remains consistent in terms of the high-quality material. For me, it's his best album since *Spectral Mornings* and one of the reasons why you are holding this book in your hand. Steve himself has said 'It's the best thing I've ever done' and confidently declared 'This album's my own Dark Side Of The Pepper'. The core members of his band and loyal regulars like Dick Driver and Christine Townsend are complimented by a host of international guest musicians with several returning from *The Night Siren*. The album is an exploration of

143

different sounds, textures and instrumentation and the end result is a rich fusion of symphonic rock and world music. The conflict between good and evil is a recurring theme and the album title alludes to Steve's concerns over the current world situation, especially the resurgence of the far-right. It could have equally been titled 'At the Edge of Darkness', but he remains optimistic about the future, while the contrast between darkness and light is a thread that weaves through the album.

The previous year, the mammoth and self-explanatory *Genesis Revisited, Solo Gems & GTR 2018 Tour de Force!* covered Canada, the USA, South America, Japan and Europe. An autumn trek around the UK followed, complete with an orchestra, a first for Steve. It was documented by the *Genesis Revisited Band & Orchestra: Live at the Royal Festival Hall* recorded in October 2018 and released twelve months later.

At the Edge of Light was almost unanimously acclaimed by both fans and critics. It reached 28 in the UK chart on 7 February 2019 and did even better in Germany and Switzerland, peaking at thirteen and 21 respectively. Around 160 shows followed and in addition to the new album, the *Genesis Revisited* Tour 2019 showcased *Selling England by the Pound* – Steve's favourite Genesis album – in its entirety and celebrated the 40th anniversary of *Spectral Mornings*. He also joined Yes on the 2019 *Cruise to the Edge*.

The cover design for *At the Edge of Light* is in the same style as the last two albums with another striking cover image and Maurizio and Angéla Vicedomini's photographic artwork illustrating each track.

'Fallen Walls and Pedestals' 2:17 (Steve Hackett, Roger King)

The opening instrumental establishes the tone of the album and is another of Steve's east meets west musical combinations. It features a strident orchestral riff and Gary O'Toole's pounding drums which inevitably bring Led Zep's 'Kashmir' to mind. The guitar work is pure Hackett, however, veering from the hard and mean to melodic without a pause. He makes good use of the guitar's onboard feedback, adding a touch of sustain and bags of finger tremolo. It's a great title that reflects on all those 'great and greedy' people that have disappeared in time but remain in the pages of history and have left a lasting legacy. Together with its companion song 'Beasts in Our Time', this was played on the 2019 tour.

'Beasts in Our Time' 6:20 (S. Hackett, Jo Hackett, King)

In keeping with the previous track, this song reflects on the evil mongers that exist in current times, influenced by the past. The title is a play on words, recalling the infamous 'Peace for our time' declaration by British prime minister Chamberlain, less than a year before the outbreak of the second world war. The closing line 'Wrecked on the rocks of the Daily Wail' is a pointed sideswipe at Britain's right-wing tabloids.

There's a sinister beauty that pervades the swaying orchestral intro, subsiding for Steve's melancholic ballad backed by acoustic guitar. Rob Townsend and John Hackett come into their own with superb and contrasting tenor sax and flute solos respectively. At 4:14, the song launches into a heavy rock shuffle with guitar doubling Jonas Reingold's propulsive bass riff which, slightly surprisingly, was written by Jo. The explosive finale is prog-metal at its bombastic best.

'Under the Eye of the Sun' 7:06 (S. Hackett, J. Hackett)

The album's most immediate song, this was the first single, released on 30 November 2018. The accompanying promo video is a photo montage from Steve and Jo's world travels including America's midwest, Petra in Jordan and Uluru in Australia. The song was largely instigated by Jo who co-wrote the lyrics and is an ode to the planet's natural wonders and the literal contrast between light and dark.

It feels like the best song the Californication incarnation of Yes never performed, boasting an exhilarating melody and bright harmonies with Steve and Amanda Lehmann's customary layered vocals. The Yes influence was perhaps a legacy from working with Chris Squire in 2012. Indeed, previously, Chris had asked Steve to join Yes. The ambient instrumental mid-section is something else again. Influenced by world music with Middle Eastern and Indian imagery, it features the eerie sound of Townsend's Duduk. Steve's majestic guitar break that follows flies like the wind with Reingold's bass and Gulli Briem's drums snapping at his heels.

'Underground Railroad' 6:22 (S. Hackett, J. Hackett, King)

This is a song with a similar theme to 'Black Thunder' on the *Wolflight* album. The Underground Railroad was a system of secret routes used by nineteenth-century American slaves to escape to a life of freedom. Steve dedicated the track to all the African-Americans that had been appallingly treated over the years. It presages the surge in the 'Black Lives Matter' movement, so prominent in the news during 2020, following the death of George Floyd.

The introduction with country flavoured dobro acoustic guitar and harmonica reeks of the American South. The song benefits from the soulful singing of sisters Durga and Lorelei McBroom, known for their stage work with Pink Floyd. They bring a gospel influence and a touch of Aretha Franklin-like soul to the song. In addition to the title, Steve's preoccupation with trains manifests itself in the steam locomotive rhythm at 2:45 courtesy of King's programming. The coda, featuring sunny harmonies and soaring guitar, brings the track – and its examination of the plight of the slaves – to a triumphant conclusion. Released on 21 December 2018, 'Underground Railroad' was the second single, released prior to the album.

'Those Golden Wings' 11:09 (S. Hackett, J. Hackett, King)

The album's centrepiece is one of Steve's most uplifting and expansive songs. Appropriately, it's an epic celebration of love in all its glory, dedicated to his kindred spirit, Jo. King really excels himself here, aided by the multi-tracked

145

string section of Christine Townsend and Dick Driver with John Hackett adding flute. The result is a rich musical confection with masterful orchestral arrangements and a touch of classical pomp.

A multifaceted song, the sweeping introduction featuring strings and harp is pure Tchaikovsky in all his romantic glory. It leads into the acoustic folky verses with twelve-string guitar and an uplifting chorus which takes Steve to his upper vocal register. At 3:52, he adds fluid classical guitar to enhance the song's classical timbre. The choral sections scale operatic heights with more than a hint of ELO's 'Mr Blue Sky' and Carl Orff's 'Carmina Burana'. The sequence at 7:45 that sounds like a massed cathedral choir in full flight is stunning. At 8:37, Steve winds things up with a grandstanding guitar solo with strong support from Nick D'Virgilio's articulate drumming.

'Shadow and Flame' 4:22 (S. Hackett, J. Hackett)
Despite the evocative lyrics – inspired by Indian culture and the waters of the river Ganges which flows through India and Bangladesh – this is a mostly instrumental track. Steve captures the contrasting qualities of India, its people and culture, using orchestral, raga and psychedelic textures. Perhaps inspired by Bollywood, it has a dense, cinematic quality. Sheema Mukherjee's virtuoso sitar playing is breathtaking, underpinned by Steve's raunchy guitar and King's relentless programmed drums. The frantic end section features three different guitar tracks playing in counterpoint, evoking the controlled chaos of India's bustling city streets.

'Hungry Years' 4:34 (S. Hackett)
This is a pop song with a good deal of charm that reflects on the wilderness years of emotional loss and fear before finding true love. It's also a nostalgic reference to 'The Hungry Years', a much-loved rock music venue in Brighton that closed in 2000. It's influenced by the American vocal harmony groups of the 1960s like The Byrds and The Mamas & the Papas, complete with a breezy melody, jangly guitars and a jaunty rhythm courtesy of Reingold and drummer Simon Phillips. Steve and Amanda duet superbly and the latter's counterpoint in the catchy choral hook adds a Fleetwood Mac vibe. She even manages to sound like Enya in the brief but haunting middle-eight at 2:07.

'Descent' 4:20 (S. Hackett)
The contrast between this and the proceeding song couldn't be more acute. 'Descent' combines with 'Conflict' and 'Peace' to form a three-part suite to conclude the album. Here, a descent into darkness leads to a battle against the forces of evil – 'Conflict' – before reaching the light at the end of the tunnel and salvation – 'Peace'. 'Descent' is a brooding, slow-burning instrumental with a rising bolero drum pattern and Mellotron-like strings that bring to mind Holst's 'Mars, The Bringer Of War'. The tortured guitar break towards the end takes sustain to new heights.

'Conflict' 2:36 (S. Hackett, King)

Another darkly atmospheric instrumental, 'Conflict' features Steve's moody lead guitar underpinned by King's restless orchestrations and rhythm track before reaching a calming conclusion.

'Peace' 5:03 (S. Hackett, J. Hackett)

'Peace' is a suitably elegiac song on which to conclude the album. It benefits from one of Steve's most sensitive vocals and a stirring melody. The massed choir-like sections from Steve and Amanda are once again stunning and his trusty Les Paul gold top provides the expressive coda. King has the final word, however, closing with an orchestral flourish. 'Peace' was another song that was blessed with a fine promo video, released in September 2019.

Related Tracks

The European 'Special Edition' CD digipak includes a DVD with Roger King's 5.1 Surround Sound mix of the album and the documentary 'Somewhere At The Edge Of Light'. The Japanese edition CD features two bonus tracks, 'Teach Yourself Valcan' and 'Roulette'.

'Teach Yourself Valcan' (S. Hackett)

As all Star Trek fans know, the title is a deliberate misspelling and a play on 'Teach Yourself Vulcan'. Both this and 'Roulette' were virtually written on the spot specifically for the Japanese release and were recorded in a single day. This is an energetic instrumental and fits in comfortably with the rest of the album.

'Roulette' (S. Hackett, Benedict Fenner)

Steve recorded this spontaneous instrumental with Ben Fenner on keyboards to provide a different dynamic to his work with King. An engineer that has worked with everyone from David Bowie to Radiohead, Fenner is no stranger to working quickly and under pressure.

Under A Mediterranean Sky (2021)
Personnel:
Steve Hackett: nylon, steel string and twelve-string guitars, charango, Iraqi oud
Roger King: keyboards, programming, orchestral arrangements
John Hackett: flute on 'Casa del Fauno'
Rob Townsend: flute on 'Casa del Fauno', soprano sax on 'The Dervish and the Djin'
Malik Mansurov: tar on 'Sirocco' and 'The Dervish and the Djin'
Arsen Petrosyan: duduk on 'The Dervish and the Djin'
Christine Townsend: violin, viola on' The Memory of Myth' and 'Andalusian Heart'
Franck Avril: oboe on 'Andalusian Heart'
Produced by: Steve Hackett, Roger King
Recorded and mixed by Roger King at Siren
Record during 2020
Release date: 22 January 2021
Record label: InsideOut Music
Highest chart places: UK: 52, USA: did not chart
Running time: 51:20

In March 2020, the Covid-19 pandemic forced Steve to abandon his touring schedule, which did at least provide the opportunity to record a new acoustic album, working closely with his long-standing collaborator Roger King. Steve had whetted fans appetites when he played a short extract during one of his regular online videos broadcast from his home studio during the Covid-19 stay-at-home restrictions in the UK. The other musicians involved are mostly Hackett regulars that played on the last studio album *At The Edge Of Light* which proceeded *Under A Mediterranean Sky* by almost exactly two years.

Despite the travel restrictions in 2020, Steve's recollections of the many places he and his wife Jo had visited in previous years provided the inspiration for this album. As the title suggests, it's a musical cruise around the Mediterranean with portraits and impressions of the picturesque lands and waters of Southern Europe, North Africa and South-West Asia. It is his first all-instrumental offering since *Tribute* in 2008, although musically, this acoustic/ orchestral concept is closer in style to the more expansive *Metamorpheus*, released in 2005.

Under A Mediterranean Sky is a showcase for Hackett's clean and fluid acoustic guitar playing supported by King's symphonic soundscapes, augmented by some traditional orchestral instruments. It alternates between lush, orchestrated tracks and solo guitar exercises, evoking classical Baroque composers like Vivaldi and Bach and Romantic maestros like Sibelius and Grieg. Ethnic instruments like the tar, duduk and oud also add an authentic Middle-Eastern flavour.

Jo Hackett and her sister Amanda Lehmann are responsible for the delightfully evocative cover image.

'Mdina (The Walled City)' 8:45 (Steve Hackett, Roger King)

Mdina in Malta – also known as the 'Silent City' – dates back more than 4,000 years and is situated on a hilltop with superb views across the island. I visited Mdina in 1987 and despite its turbulent history, it has a timeless, unspoilt charm.

It opens with a roll of timpani, followed by King's dramatic keyboard orchestrations in a neo-classical/film music style that brings The Enid to mind. Steve's Spanish guitar enters the spirit with cascading note clusters, the first of many impressive solos on the album. The coda, with its lush keyboard strings, brings to mind the romantic style of Debussy and Ravel.

'Adriatic Blue' 4:51 (S. Hackett)

Inspired by the colourful, sun-dappled waters that separate the east Italian coastline and the Balkans, this is a tranquil classical guitar sonata. Steve perfectly captures the ambience of a long hot summer's day with the guitar strings rippling gently like the calm waters of the sea itself.

'Sirocco' 5:13 (S. Hackett, Jo Hackett, King)

'Sirocco' is the name given to the Mediterranean wind that blows across from the sands of the Sahara desert. This piece was inspired by a trip to Egypt and like the Sirocco, it's a very changeable piece of music. To begin with, the atmosphere is calm with Spanish guitar underpinned by gentle keyboard strings. Percussion enters at around the two-minute mark and the mood becomes more restless with a grandiose orchestral sequence capturing the majesty of North Africa, recalling Maurice Jarre's evocative film score for *Lawrence Of Arabia*.

'Joie de Vivre' 3:42 (S. Hackett, J. Hackett)

'Joie de Vivre' – enjoyment of life – is an appropriate title for this exuberant and intricate acoustic guitar workout that's probably my favourite solo guitar piece on the album. It's very reminiscent of Mason Williams' guitar instrumental 'Classical Gas' that topped the American singles chart back in 1968. Steve performed 'Classical Gas' on the 'Acoustic Trio Tour' in 2005, and even now, it demonstrates that his acoustic guitar dexterity remains undiminished, despite the fact that he celebrated his 70th birthday in 2020.

'The Memory of Myth' 3:29 (S. Hackett, J. Hackett, King)

Christine Townsend's lyrical violin solo opens 'The Memory of Myth', a track evocative of Greece and its rich history. Delicate classical guitar gives way to brooding keyboard orchestrations with a snatch of ringing mandolin like-guitar, adding a folky ambience.

'Scarlatti Sonata' 3:40 (Domenico Scarlatti)

The only non-original composition on the album, the meditative 'Scarlatti Sonata' is a solo guitar piece based on a keyboard sonata by early eighteenth-century Italian composer Domenico Scarlatti. In the Baroque style of his day, Scarlatti specialised in piano and harpsichord works, although his music was often influenced by Spanish guitar, an aspect that wouldn't have been lost on Steve when he arranged this piece.

'Casa del Fauno' 3:51 (S. Hackett, King)

The beautiful gardens and remains of the House of the Faun are located in Pompeii, Italy and date back to the second century BC. Once a striking private residence, miraculously, it partially survived the eruption of Mount Vesuvius that destroyed Pompeii in AD79. One of the album's most evocative tracks, King's romantic keys strings simmer beneath classical guitar while John Hacket and Rob Townsend provide the playful counterpoint flutes. It is absolutely superb.

'The Dervish and the Djin' 4:57 (S. Hackett, J. Hackett, King)

'Djin' is an alternative spelling for 'Djinn' if I'm not mistaken, an ancient Arabian and Islamic word for mythological spirits, demons and genies. This is the album's most dramatic track, capturing the unrest and conflicts between the middle-eastern countries to the east of the Mediterranean. Two of the musicians involved – Malik Mansurov and Arsen Petrosyan – hail from Azerbaijan and Armenia respectively, both of which border Iran. The haunting sound of the duduk is followed by the sitar-like tar and strident orchestrations that develop into a war-like march overlaid with expressive soprano sax soloing.

'Lorato' 2:29 (S. Hackett)

'Lorato' is a lilting classical guitar solo that originally featured on the 2016 charity album *Harmony For Elephants*. In addition to Steve, the various artists on the album include that other ex-Genesis guitarist Anthony Phillips. In the Tswana language spoken by certain indigenous people in Africa, 'Lorato' means 'love' or 'affection', very apt for this delightful little tune.

'Andalusian Heart' 5:34 (S. Hackett, J. Hackett, King)

Southern Spain is a region much loved by Steve, thus explaining the title of the penultimate track. He was also inspired by the flamenco guitarists and the free spirit of the gipsies that populate the region.' Andalusian Heart' has a distinctly romantic flavour and is another album highlight. Shimmering strings and airy woodwind introduce a nimble Spanish guitar solo, embellished by a sweeping orchestral finale.

'The Call of the Sea' 4:44 (S. Hackett)

For the final track, Steve's tasteful nylon guitar playing is complemented by King's restrained classical orchestrations, evoking the ebb and flow of the ocean. A flurry of rapid guitar chords in the earlier part of the piece, are calmed by the soothing keys strings, combining gracefully to bring the album to a serene conclusion.

Collaborations

This chapter includes albums where Steve has featured prominently in equal partnership with the other artists involved. In addition to those discussed here, Steve has made guest appearances on over 50 albums for various artists including Eddie Hardin, John Wetton, Steven Wilson, Billy Sherwood and Alan Parsons. His first was in 1973 on *Two Sides of Peter Banks* by the ex-Yes guitarist, an album which also featured Phil Collins. He has also guested on solo albums by his live band members including John Hackett, Nick Magnus, Dik Cadbury and Pete Hicks, and Nad Sylvan. Steve has never worked with any members of the 1970s era Genesis outside the band beyond *Voyage Of The Acolyte*.

GTR – GTR (LP: July 1986, CD: 2001)

Ten years earlier, the teaming of Steve Hackett and Steve Howe would have been a prog-head's idea of heaven. In the corporate rock world of the mid-1980s however, it proved to be a different story. While GTR were often compared to Asia and the West Coast version of Yes, their rather more formulaic, pop-prog sound was closer to American bands like Styx and REO Speedwagon despite being a British quintet (or indeed a sextet on stage).

The catchy single 'When the Heart Rules the Mind' and eponymous album were both US hits in 1986, reaching fourteen and eleven respectively. The latter suffers from Geoff Downes' overly compressed production which reduces the otherwise distinct guitar styles into a brittle pop/metal hybrid. As a result, the solo offerings 'Sketches In the Sun' and 'Hackett to Bits' seem almost out of place. Downes blamed the two guitarists, claiming they were reluctant to record together, while Hackett himself cited outside interference. However, the band acquit themselves well and frontman Max Bacon was born to sing this style of material. The guitar riff at 4:20 in 'Imagining', by the way, always reminds me of the orchestral theme in Paul McCartney & Wings' 'Live and Let Die'.

GTR's true capabilities were evident live, as captured on the *King Biscuit Flower Hour Presents GTR*, recorded in LA on 19 July 1986 and released in 1997. Feeling artistically compromised and the band beset with financial problems, Hackett jumped ship in 1987. Robert Berry was recruited to work with Howe and the band on a proposed second album and although demos were recorded, it failed to materialise.

John Hackett Steve Hackett – Sketches of Satie (CD: 8 May 2000)

Although Steve and John have been involved in numerous collaborations including guesting on each other's albums and in each other's stage appearances, this is the only album to date credited to both brothers. They have a shared love of the music of French composer Erik Satie who influenced

Steve's own compositions 'Kim' and 'The Toast'. For anyone familiar with Steve's classical albums, especially *Momentum,* this recording will hold few surprises. It contains twenty skillfully and delicately performed Satie pieces transcribed from the piano to nylon guitar and flute. This required Steve to detune his guitar and the music Is mostly a showcase for John's virtuoso flute talents with Steve's guitar providing support.

Squackett – A Life Within A Day (CD, LP: 28 May 2012, CD/ DVD: 4 June 2012)

In 2007, Steve guested on the Christmas album *Chris Squire's Swiss Choir,* a rare solo recording by the Yes bassist. It provided the catalyst for their later work together including this, their only collaborative album. Squackett – an amalgamation of Squire and Hackett – features several of Steve's regular musicians including keyboardist, producer Roger King and Amanda Lehmann on backing vocals. The title track also features Christine Townsend (viola, violin), Richard Stewart (cello) and Dick Driver (double bass). Session drummer Jeremy Stacey – who also played on *Genesis Revisited II* released the same year – completes the line-up.

The songs were mostly co-written by Steve, Chris and Roger and with the two main protagonists living on opposite sides of the Atlantic, the album had a long gestation period. On its release, many commented – wrongly – that it was more Hackett than Squire while others drew comparisons – for obvious reasons – with GTR. True, it does have an AOR sheen, but the radio-friendly tunes, fulsome harmonies, Steve's trademark guitar and Chris' signature bass rumbles are a fine combination. It also occasionally tips its hat to the likes of Led Zeppelin, Pink Floyd and Yes. An edited version of 'Sea of Smiles' b/w 'Perfect Love Song' was released as a single on 21 April 2012. The song 'Stormchaser' had previously been performed by Steve during the early part of his 2009 European tour.

Steve Hackett & Djabe – Summer Storms & Rocking Rivers (CD/DVD:2013)
Djabe & Steve Hackett – Life Is A Journey: The Sardinia Tapes (2 CD: 2017)
Djabe & Steve Hackett – Life Is A Journey: The Budapest Live Tapes (2 CD/DVD: 2018)
Djabe & Steve Hackett – Back To Sardinia (CD/DVD:2019)

Steve has performed on stage with Hungarian jazz-fusion band Djabe many times, and they recorded several jointly credited albums. *Summer Storms & Rocking Rivers* is a combination of two live shows, Bratislava in July 2011 and Budapest in November 2012. The sets feature a selection of songs from Steve, Genesis and Djabe. *The Sardinia* Tapes is the results of an improvised session recorded in 2016 near the Nostra Signora di Tergu cathedral on the island of Sardinia. *The Budapest Live Tapes* is a concert from October 2017. Steve is on stage for the second half of the set performing his solo and Genesis material. In 2019, Djabe returned to the cathedral location for *Back To Sardinia* although Steve recorded his parts later in Budapest.

Steve has also featured as a 'special guest' on the Djabe albums *Sipi Emlékkoncert – Sipi Benefit Concert* (2009), *In the Footsteps of Attila and Genghis* (2011), *Live in Blue* (2014) and *It Is Never the Same Twice* (2018). They provide the opportunity to express himself purely through his guitar playing without the responsibility of fronting the band or writing the music. A desire to expand his musical horizons – embracing world music and modern classical for example – also led to him working with Icelandic rock band Todmobile and Italian composer Marco Lo Muscio amongst others.

Live Albums and Videos

Although Steve toured consistently from October 1978 onwards, his first official live recording – a video – didn't see the light of day until 1992. The new millennium has seen a plethora of live albums, especially following the release of the *Genesis Revisited II* studio album in 2012. The majority of Steve's live output on both audio and video boasts excellent recordings and performances, especially those recorded post-2010.

Steve Hackett Live (VHS: 1992)
Steve's first video was recorded at Central TV Studios, Nottingham in October 1990. The 55-minute set favours his own material with Genesis' 'In That Quiet Earth' included for good measure. The band comprises Steve (guitar, vocals), John Hackett (guitar, flute, bass pedals), Julian Colbeck (keyboards, vocals), Ian Ellis (bass, vocals) and Fudge Smith (drums).

Time Lapse (CD: 31 July 1992)
Steve's first live CD cherrypicks seven tracks from *Steve Hackett Live* and adds seven from the earlier *Cured* tour – recorded at the Savoy Theater, New York in November 1981. For the NY performance, Steve and John are joined by Nick Magnus (keyboards), Chas Cronk (bass, vocals) and Ian Mosley (drums). It boasts a strong representation of tracks from his first four classic studio albums.

There Are Many Sides to the Night (CD: 1995)
This is a semi-acoustic performance featuring Steve on classical guitar and Julian Colbeck on keyboards. It was recorded at the Teatro Metropolitan, Palermo, Sicily in December 1994. In addition to solo classical pieces, this superbly performed and recorded 70-minute set includes some of Steve's better-known tunes unplugged, plus a beautiful version of Ennio Morricone's timeless 'Cinema Paradiso'.

The Tokyo Tapes (2 CD: 1998, DVD: 2001, 2CD/DVD: 2013)
Taken from two shows filmed at Koseinenkin Hall, Tokyo on 16 & 17 December 1996, the definite version is the 2013 2CD/DVD reissue. The starry line-up features Steve (guitar, vocals), John Wetton (bass, vocals), Chester Thompson (drums), Ian McDonald (flute, saxophone, keyboards) and Julian Colbeck (keyboards). The crowd-pleasing 100-minute setlist includes songs by Genesis, King Crimson, Asia, Steve and John.

Live Archive 70, 80, 90s (4 CD: 12 November 2001)
Spanning three decades, this 4 CD set features separate shows recorded at London's Hammersmith Odeon on 30 June 1979, Rome's Castel Sant'Angelo on 13 September 1981 and London's The Grand Theatre on 8 June 1993.

Although several of the tracks such as 'Clocks' are duplicated, it's Steve's most comprehensive live package to date. The first two discs showcase the near two-hour Hammersmith Odeon gig in its entirety.

Live Archive 70s Newcastle (CD: 2001)

Despite the title, in addition to songs recorded at Newcastle's City Hall on 26 October 1979, the last three tracks were recorded at London's Hammersmith Odeon on 30 October 1978. This was a bonus disc with the original release of *Live Archive 70, 80, 90s.*

Somewhere in South America... Live in Buenos Aires (2CD, DVD/2CD: 19 November 2002)

Filmed at the Teatro Coliseo on 1 July 2001, the DVD is an indispensable addition to any Hackett collection. Steve, Roger King, Rob Townsend, Terry Gregory and Gary O'Toole charge their way through a winning selection of gems like 'Serpentine Song', 'Watcher of the Skies', 'Firth of Fifth' and 'Riding the Colossus'.

Hungarian Horizons: Live In Budapest (DVD/2CD: 1 September 2003, 2CD: 27 October 2003)

Another excellent package, this 'Acoustic Trio' concert featuring Steve on guitar, John on flute and Roger King on keyboards was recorded on 26 January 2002. The performance and recording are faultless as is the near two-hour set, combining tastefully arranged versions of Genesis and Hackett, plus some traditional pieces.

Live Archive NEARfest (2CD: 28 June 2003)

This is another fine release from the 'Live Archives' series. It includes the complete show recorded at Patriots Theater, Trenton, New Jersey on 30 June 2002. The setlist is very similar to that of *Somewhere In South America* with the substitution of the evergreens 'Spectral Mornings' and 'Every Day'.

Horizons (DVD: 2003)

A DVD reissue of the *Steve Hackett Live* video as part of the 'Classic Rock Legends' series. The Roger Dean inspired artwork is very different from the original.

Once Above A Time (DVD: 2004)

The well-oiled machine of Steve, King, Townsend, Gregory and O'Toole breeze their way through a Genesis / Hackett 'greatest hits' set filmed at Budapest's Petőfi Csarnok on 3 April 2004. They were touring in support of *To Watch The Storms* and five songs from the album were played during this complete, near two-hour, show.

Live Legends (DVD: 2004)

A repackaged, reissue of *Horizons*, aka *Steve Hackett Live*. With some songs segueing into others, they are not all listed which makes for unreliable comparisons between each version.

Live Archive 03 (2 CD: 2004)

Like the *Once Above A Time* DVD, this compilation of tracks was recorded during the *To Watch The Storms* tour. This, however, was the 2003 European leg, and the repertoire is substantially different. Although there are similarities to the *Live Archive NEARfest* setlist, it's still a worthwhile release.

Live Archive 04 (2 CD: 28 June 2004)

This, on the other hand, is a complete audio version of the *Once Above A Time* show.

Live Archive 05 (2CD: 23 August 2005)

Similar to *Hungarian Horizons,* this features the 'Acoustic Trio' of Steve, John and Roger. It was recorded in April 2005 to promote the *Metamorpheus* album released the same month. The first part of the set is solo classical guitar, joined by flute and keyboards for the more satisfying second section, which features perennials like 'Hairless Heart' and 'Ace of Wands'.

Spectral Mornings (DVD: 29 August 2005)

Steve's earliest performance on DVD features highlights from the first three studio albums including 'Ace of Wands', 'Narnia' and – naturally – 'Spectral Mornings'. It was recorded for the German TV series *Musikladen* on 8 November 1978, with the then-band Steve, John, Nick Magnus, Dik Cadbury, John Shearer and Pete Hicks on great form. Considering the vintage, the picture and sound are very good.

Live Archive 83 (CD: 17 June 2006)

Another acoustic set, this is Steve and John paired down to a duet. It dates back to 4 November 1983 and was recorded at the Queen's Hall, Edinburgh to promote *Bay of Kings*. A healthy selection of pieces from that album are performed, along with rearranged versions of instrumentals like 'Jacuzzi'.

Live Rails (2CD: 25 April 2011)

A popular album with fans, this is a compilation of recordings from the 2009-2010 *Out of the Tunnel's Mouth* tour. Featuring the line-up of Steve, Roger King, Amanda Lehmann, Nick Beggs, Rob Townsend and Gary O'Toole, there is again a harmonious marriage of Genesis and Hackett tunes with the emphasis on his earlier material.

Fire & Ice (DVD: 25 September 2011)

On 30 November 2010, the same line-up as *Live Rails* took to the stage at London's Shepherds Bush Empire during the *Around the World in Eighty Trains tour.* Filmed in its entirety, the near two hour and thirty-minute set packs a lot in, with guest John Wetton singing 'All Along the Watchtower' and Steven Wilson adding his guitar talents to two songs.

Genesis Revisited: Live at Hammersmith (3 CD/2 DVD: 18 November 2013)

This is the first of the lavish box-sets that would become Steve's speciality in the 2010s. It was also his first live album to enter the UK chart, reaching 58. Nick Beggs is replaced by Lee Pomeroy on bass, Nad Sylvan is the lead singer and guests include Nik Kershaw, Steve Rothery, John Wetton and Jakko Jakszyk. Recorded at London's Hammersmith Apollo on 10 May 2013, the set is composed of songs from the two *Genesis Revisited* studio albums.

The Bremen Broadcast (DVD: 28 October 2013)

A repackaged reissue of the 2005 *Spectral Mornings* DVD. The title is a reference to the Radio Bremen studios where the 1978 session took place. The cover pic of Steve is from the back of the *Spectral Mornings* album sleeve which was released six months after this recording was made.

Genesis Revisited: Live at the Royal Albert Hall (2 CD/2 DVD/ Blu-ray: 30 June 2014, 3 LP/2 CD: 12 June 2020)

The same line-up as *Live at Hammersmith* is joined by guests John Wetton, Ray Wilson and Roine Stolt. Recorded on 24 October 2013 in London's most prestigious venue, many of the songs in the 135-minute set are replicated from that album. It was remastered and reissued in 2020 specifically for vinyl lovers.

Access All Areas (CD/DVD: 2014)

Yet another repackaged reissue of *Steve Hackett Live,* aka *Horizons,* aka *Live Legends.*

The Total Experience Live in Liverpool (2 CD/2 DVD & Blu-ray: 24 June 2016)

The subtitle 'Acolyte to Wolflight with Genesis Classics' tells you all you need to know about this box-set. Roine Stolt takes over bass and twelve-string guitar duties while John Hackett and Amanda Lehmann are listed as guests. The 150-minute set was recorded at The Liverpool Philharmonic Hall on 23 October 2015.

The Total Experience Live In Japan (2 CD: 12 October 2016)

This was officially released in Japan only and limited to 1,500 copies. It was recorded at Club Citta in Kawasaki, Japan on 21 May 2016. The setlist is almost the same as *The Total Experience Live in Liverpool,* minus 'Jacuzzi' and 'After The Ordeal'. For the encore, 'Clocks' is replaced with 'Dance on a Volcano'. Nick Beggs returns on bass and twelve-string and John and Amanda do not take part.

Wuthering Nights: Live in Birmingham (2 CD/2 DVD, 2 CD, 2 DVD/Blu-ray: 26 January 2018)

This album was recorded on 1 May 2017 at Birmingham's Symphony Hall during the *Wind & Wuthering* 40th anniversary tour. Five songs from the album were played, along with 'Inside and Out' and several of Steve's solo tunes. The line-up is Steve, King, Sylvan, O'Toole, Townsend, Beggs and 'special guests', John and Amanda.

Genesis Revisited Band & Orchestra: Live at the Royal Festival Hall (2 CD/Blu-ray: 25 October 2019)

The band – with Jonas Reingold on bass – are supplemented by the 41-piece Heart Of England Orchestra conducted by Bradley Thachuk. Recorded on 4 October 2018, in addition to early Genesis staples like 'Supper's Ready' and 'The Musical Box', Steve also includes songs from his more recent studio albums.

Selling England by the Pound & Spectral Mornings: Live at Hammersmith (2CD/DVD, 2CD/Blu-ray, 4LP/2CD, 2CD/DVD/Blu-ray: 25th September 2020)

As it says on the cover, this features two of Steve's favourite albums, released in multiple formats. Recorded in November 2019, Craig Blundell replaces O'Toole on drums, otherwise it's the same band as *Live at the Royal Festival Hall* – minus the orchestra. *Selling England by the Pound* is performed in its entirety along with most of *Spectral Mornings* and highlights from the latest album *At the Edge of Light.* The performances and the recording quality are excellent.

Compilations and Documentaries

Despite a prolific output spanning five decades, Steve has been favoured with only a handful of compilation albums.

The Unauthorised Biography (CD: 26 October 1992)

Surprisingly, Steve chose to populate his first compilation with mostly lesser-known songs rather than stage favourites. As a result, delights like 'The Virgin and the Gipsy', 'Hammer in the Sand' and 'Hoping Love Will Last' are included. The two previously unreleased tracks 'Don't Fall Away From Me' and 'Prayers and Dreams' are discussed in the *Guitar Noir* chapter.

Guitare Classique (CD: 2001)

A handy – but not easy to find – CD for anyone that's missed out on Steve's classical albums. It includes tracks from the acoustic live album *There Are Many Sides to the Night*, the *Sketches of Satie* collaboration with John and *A Midsummer Night's Dream*.

Genesis Files (2CD: February 2002)

A slightly misleading title. Although it includes virtually every track from the 1996 *Genesis Revisited* album, there are also several from *The Tokyo Tapes*, two from *Bay Of Kings* and the odd one from *Darktown* and *Feedback 86*. The latter two have no connection with Genesis at all.

Premonitions: The Charisma Recordings 1975-1983 (10 CD/4 DVD: 16 October 2015)

Steve's most lavish box-set to date. The CDs feature his first six albums with the occasional bonus track, live recordings – some previously unreleased – and Steven Wilson stereo remixes of *Please Don't Touch!* and *Spectral Mornings*. The DVDs provide 5.1 Surround mixes of the first four albums. This package is well worth having for those looking to upgrade the original vinyl releases.

Steve Hackett – The Man, The Music (DVD: 16 October 2015)

As it says on the tin, this 140-minute documentary is dedicated to Steve, his life and his music. It covers his career in depth with insight from the man himself along with collaborators like Roger King, Chris Squire and – of course – his brother John.

5 Classic Albums (5 CD: 13 May 2016)

The title is mostly justified, featuring the first four studio albums plus *Highly Strung* – and curiously not *Cured* – in a handy package. Part of the budget 'Classic Albums' series, they have not been remastered and do not include bonus tracks.

Broken Skies Outspread Wings 1984-2006 (6 CD/2DVD: 5 October 2018)

This picks up from where *Premonitions* left off. The CDs are devoted to *Till We Have Faces, Feedback 86, Guitar Noir, Darktown, To Watch The Storms* and *Wild Orchids* in their entirety. The DVDs offer 5.1 mixes of a selection of songs, the *Somewhere in South America* concert film plus backstage and interview footage from 2000. Like *Premonitions*, it boasts new artwork and a logo by Roger Dean.

Online Resources

Hackettsongs.com – Steve's official website

Thegenesisarchive.co.uk – Archival resource including Steve's solo work

Genesis-news.com – Fan website on all things Genesis including solo releases

Dprp.net – Reviews website with in-depth coverage of Steve's solo output